Viral Literature:
Alone Together in Georgia

"This is an inspiring work of the populist imagination, in the best senses of both 'populist' and 'imagination.' Some thirty plus works of narrative and poetic resourcefulness offer a range of responses to the early months of the pandemic. It's far more than a set of laments; we find here a vigorous and hopeful treasury of lives lived in those dark months of 2020, along with broader histories and geographies that locate the experience within what proves to be the very lively territory of Georgians' creativity."

–Professor Leonard Barkan,
Professor of Comparative Literature, Princeton University

"I confess to reading this book out of order, flipping first to entries written by authors I already knew—Kay, Musser, Ray, Ramsey, Rawlings. I savored their contributions and then worked through those by authors I wasn't yet familiar with—poets and writers such as Cardenas, White, Salcedo, Kamal and Black—and found the same quality of thought, of introspection, and an ability to inform and entertain using the written word. The compiler of this diverse, entertaining book (fiction and non-fiction; poetry and prose) hoped to provide readers with meaningful, topical material during an exceptional pandemic. He succeeded splendidly."

–Daniel M. Roper,
Publisher and Editor, *Georgia Backroads* magazine

"*Viral Literature* does what I'd always hoped the Decatur Book Festival would do… document the wild, glorious, and diverse abundance of talent that calls this region home. Together, these pieces tell the story of this place and time, but it also demonstrates the strength of this community of writers."

—Daren Wang,
Founder of the AJC Decatur Book Festival
and author of *The Hidden Light of Northern Fires*

Viral Literature

On Assignment
Pg 91
Flip it in the Butt
Pg 73

Scott Thomas Outlaw

Janisse Ray *

Share Your Thoughts

Want to help make *Viral Literature* a bestselling book? Consider leaving an honest review of this book on Goodreads, on your personal author website or blog, and anywhere else readers go for recommendations. It's our priority at SFK Press to publish books for readers to enjoy, and our authors appreciate and value your feedback.

Our Southern Fried Guarantee

If you wouldn't enthusiastically recommend one of our books with a 4- or 5-star rating to a friend, then the next story is on us. We believe that much in the stories we're telling. Simply email us at pr@sfkmultimedia.com.

SFK
PRESS

Viral

Literature

Alone Together in Georgia

Stories from 2020 Quarantine

Edited by

Clayton H. Ramsey

*In honor of those who healed, delivered, served, created,
taught, and endured during the pandemic of our time,
and in memory of those who were lost.*

Contents

Preface

PLAGUE, THE UNCHECKED RAMPAGE OF VIRUS THROUGH human populations, has been memorialized through the centuries. Historical accounts impressed on clay tablets and recorded in YouTube videos preserve the witness of every culture from ancient Babylon to current nations strafed by COVID-19 to this constantly evolving and viciously persistent threat to life, welfare, and civilization. Religious texts like the Hebrew Torah, recording Egyptian pestilence as part of a divine stratagem to free God's people, have tried to place the experience of disease and death in theological contexts that offer philosophical meaning to the suffering. In addition to historians and theologians, poets and storytellers have also applied their craft to representing and understanding the drama of infections that tear through bodies and societies. Books like Daniel Defoe's *A Journal of the Plague Year* (1722), about the Great Plague of London, which he calls the "Great Visitation," in 1665; Katherine Anne Porter's *Pale Horse, Pale Rider* (1939), about the 1918 Influenza Epidemic; and Albert Camus's *The Plague* (1947), about the illness ripping through the French Algerian city of Oran, are several of the more well-known and recent literary depictions of plague. But preceding them is one by a 14th-century Florentine writer, Giovanni Boccaccio.

A medieval history class in college introduced me to Boccaccio's delightful *The Decameron* (1353). One of the "Three Crowns of Florence," along with Dante Alighieri and Francesco Petrarca, or Petrarch, Boccaccio was the illegitimate son of a merchant in Florence. Born in 1313, his life straddled the middle years of the century that bridged the worldview of the Middle Ages and the humanistic blossoming of the Renaissance. Careening between banking and the law, he eventually settled into the niche of poetry, and it was in this creative vocation where he shone most brightly.

Whereas Dante dazzled with the breathtaking sublimity of eternity and Petrarch inspired with the poetry of his *canzonieri*, Boccaccio was a master entertainer, and his most enjoyable work charms with the pure fun of good storytelling.

Beginning in 1347, the Black Death descended on Western Europe. Tucked away in the digestive tract of the Oriental rat flea, the *coccobacillus* bacterium *Yersinia pestis* found a means of transmission in rodents and a host in humans, where it invaded vulnerable lymph glands and multiplied, creating the painful and grotesque black buboes that gave the disease its name. Boccaccio saw the devastation in his native Florence, and, as the scythe of the Reaper cut down tens of millions on the continent, he chose to confront the nihilism and despair of the event with art. The brilliant result of his skill was *The Decameron*. It is a "frame story"— stories nestled in stories. His premise was the escape of ten young people from the pestilential Florence in the 1340s. The cohort of friends, seven women and three men, found a country villa on the outskirts of town, and there they endured a self-imposed quarantine, safe, they believed, from the reach of disease. While they were in isolation, they sang and danced and ate and told stories. Each one told one story on a theme every day for ten days—a total of 100 stories. The title *The Decameron* is itself eponymous, a representation of the frame, as a Greek word for "ten days." It would be known as *La Commedia Umana*, "The Human Comedy," in contrast to Dante's masterpiece, and was written a full five hundred years before Balzac's *magnum opus* of the same name.

Originally written in an accessible Tuscan vernacular, and not the Latin of church and state, the stories explore love, fortune, and trickery. They are tragic, comic, and farcical; light and philosophical. They were born of confinement but without the piety of the cloister— earthy, bawdy, silly, and serious. Prof. Leonard Barkan, Princeton University's Class of 1943 University Professor and Chair of the Department of Comparative Literature, called it "the greatest short story collection of all time" in Wayne Rebhorn's 2013 English translation. Among many others, Chaucer, Shakespeare, and Keats all felt the effects of these tales and kneaded them into their canonical works. Generations of readers have been delighted and enlightened by them no less than these masters.

When the novel coronavirus spread from Wuhan, China, to envelop the globe in early 2020, I was reminded of Boccaccio and his magnificent attempt to face spreading, highly infectious disease with stories. Storytelling, he reminded me, makes us human and gives us connection and meaning when society is unraveling, especially when a virus is ripping through communities and human life seems especially tenuous. When the world is in peril and many of us, like the young Florentines, have been trapped in our homes, what we have turned to for intellectual stimulation, emotional comfort, distraction, and even hope has been art. We've read novels. We've binge-watched Netflix. We've listened to music. We may have even taken up a pen or brush and created our own art. Boccaccio the storyteller had his characters tell stories in confinement. And the joy, laughter, and reflection of these tales has echoed for almost seven hundred years. They are the luminous traces of the indomitable human spirit saved for the ages, and they still have the potential to inspire and delight us.

Moved by Boccaccio's example, though not exactly duplicating his literary plan, I reached out to some of the most talented writers in the state of Georgia. Thirty-two of them agreed to submit work to this anthology. Twenty are from the wider creative community, five were selected from among the 1,000 members of the Atlanta Writers Club, and seven were the top winners of a special AWC contest. They are novelists, short-story writers, poets, playwrights, historians, academics, and journalists, with even one cartoonist to represent the visual arts. We gave them the theme of "Alone Together in Georgia" and a page limit and told them to let their imaginations and creativity run free between these two boundaries. The result, as you will see, was remarkable, our best attempt to honor Boccaccio and hopefully inject some relief and optimism into an otherwise grim moment in our history.

My special thanks to the Board of Directors of the Atlanta Writers Club for their approval and support of the project; to

Viral Literature: Alone Together in Georgia

George Weinstein, current AWC president and novelist, an early and consistent backer of this effort, for his encouragement and assistance; and to Steve McCondichie, publisher and owner of SFK Press, for his generosity of time, resources, and expertise. The writers in the anthology are not only fabulous writers, they are also extraordinary human beings. Without their involvement, cooperation, talent, and good cheer, this collection would have been greatly impoverished and likely limited to a four-page introduction. I am fortunate to count friends among them and remain grateful for their help breathing life into a medieval idea.

The National Historic Landmark Wren's Nest, home of Joel Chandler Harris and preserver of the art of storytelling in west Atlanta, and Literacy Action, Inc., described as the "oldest, largest, and leading adult basic education nonprofit in the Southeastern United States," will split the royalties and revenues from the sale of this collection. We are all thrilled that two such worthy charities will be the recipients of the income from this project.

By the time this book finds you, the storm may have passed or darkened. Whenever you read it, we trust it will buoy you. We hope you cry and laugh and think and fill up the empty, hurting places in you with these words from thirty-two fertile hearts and minds to yours. As we count the days until this crisis has passed, I wish you and those you cherish health, safety, and a way to find peace and comfort. May these stories and poems help along the way.

—CLAYTON H. RAMSEY
Atlanta Writers Club Officer Emeritus
and VP of Contests, Awards & Scholarships
May 15, 2020

Foreword

IF YOU'RE READING THIS DURING THE COVID-19 PANDEMIC, we hope this anthology will provide you with comfort, big questions to ponder, some humor, and, above all, entertainment to help you through this tragic, chaotic time. If you're reading this post-pandemic, perhaps you look back on that time and feel a mixture of grief over the losses and vanished opportunities, wonder at the global reach of such a microscopic nemesis, and maybe a bit of nostalgia about sheltering for months with loved ones or cherished pastimes.

The pace of life has seemed to slow considerably during the long period of being alone together. Some of us have rediscovered birdsongs and the beauty of the infinite night sky. Some have marched, protested, and agitated to call out injustice from behind masks. There has been time enough at last to read, learn a craft or skill, and sit with one's emotions and memories. Others have connected more deeply than ever with their families—either under the same roof or online.

To me and at least some of the contributing authors of this work, writing during the pandemic feels a little like making a diary entry during a war, when the outcome is far from certain and the news seems to go from bad to worse. The person writing such an entry doesn't know whether he or she will be touched directly by the scourge or whether family or friends will be affected. All the diarist knows is the present circumstance: hoping for the best while bracing for the worst.

If that analogy strikes you as too dire or melodramatic, here is another way some of our authors consider the anthology in light of the current moment: those of us contributing pieces are a bit like the proverbial shipwreck survivor stranded on a desert island, putting a message in a bottle and casting it into the waves. We have no idea who will read what we've written or when that might be. All we can do is convey our thoughts and feelings, tell our stories and our truths, and hope the bottle holds together and some reader in need finds what we've written. Rather than seeking rescue ourselves, we hope that our words will save that reader in some small way. Perhaps we can evoke a long-dormant emotion, provide nourishment for their mind or soul, or inspire them to put their own message in a bottle and cast it from their place of isolation to be received by another reader in need, renewing the cycle again and again.

We hope you enjoy this collection of bottled messages gathered from the sea of imagination by the Atlanta Writers Club, which was founded in 1914, a few years before the previous pandemic. Herein, well-known contributors from Georgia are joined by local favorites and some authors who are being published for the first time. Together, we share a love of the written word and a desire to make an impact on readers. Prepare to be moved emotionally, intellectually, and soulfully.

If you're reading this during the pandemic, we hope for the best for you and yours. If you're reading this post-pandemic, we're glad you made it through the storm.

—GEORGE WEINSTEIN
Executive Director & Acting President, Atlanta Writers Club
AtlantaWritersClub.org
July 14, 2020

Text TOON to 22828 for a daily dose of Man Overboard

TERRY KAY

The Strange Dance of the White Dog

W HITE DOG CAME STARVING. JUST APPEARED ONE DAY, as dogs will.

My father saw her from the middle room window. She was at the backdoor steps, where there'd been grease dripped from frying pans my mother had taken across the yard to pour out at the edge of the pasture. There was not much left of the grease—my mother having died weeks earlier—but White Dog licked hungrily at the spots, licked the blood out of her tongue on the cement steps, she was so starved.

A stray, my father thought. A skinny beggar dog wandering back-yards for scraps left by pets too well-fed to fight. Skittish, from the looks of her. Maybe locked up too long by somebody mean enough to do such things. Maybe picked up the rabies somewhere. Best to run her off. Not let her get used to food for the taking.

My father was on his walker then, balancing on one fairly good leg and four stems of aluminum, pulling along like a slow metal spider. He would be no match for White Dog if it was a case of rabies, but he had pride (and remembered muscles), and there was a beautiful stubbornness in the way he wanted to do things for himself. When he could not chase the dog away by shouting from behind the screen door, he pushed his way outside and got his weight under his good leg and took his walker and jabbed it at White Dog like some ancient animal trainer in a traveling carnival, and White Dog jumped and whimpered and ducked her head and crawled away under the house, only to show up later, begging with sad eyes at some safe distance.

This went on for days, the shouting and jabbing and whimpering and retreating and reappearing, but White Dog would not leave, and my father said to Fred, my brother-in-law, "Somebody ought to take a gun and put that starving dog out of her misery." And Fred, who knew my father well (knew he was asking, not discussing), said he'd do it first chance he got.

"Somebody ought to," my father repeated philosophically. "I'd do it myself, but I can't hold a gun leaning on this thing. Anyhow, my eye's gone for shooting."

So was his heart. He couldn't kill animals then, at his age, and the walker had nothing to do with it. He'd had to kill too many in his years. Stall and feed-lot animals, pasture animals. Cows and pigs he'd grown from newborns trembling unsteadily in the womb-steam of their mothers, their wet faces slapping instinctively at swollen milk teats—animals he'd named and petted until they'd followed him around like puppies. And then he'd have to put a gun to their heads and kill them for food. Over the years, he'd had enough of it. (I think that is the way it was with White Dog, why he had to call on Fred to do the killing.)

Maybe my father got to thinking about all of that. Maybe he got to thinking that he'd killed out of need and, as it sometimes happens, out of habit. But he had no need to kill White Dog, except out of mercy, and, besides, he had enough to eat to share with a dog, now that no one was left at home but him, and he didn't eat much, working as little as he did.

And there was the other thing—as he later told me: It played on his mind that White Dog had appeared only a short time after my mother had died, about the same time the grievers had begun leaving him alone. Strange, it happening that way. Him being alone. Nothing to do but watch television and sit in his rocker beside his rolltop desk and, at night, laboriously write in his journal of fragments of memories. And then White Dog, white as an apparition. Eyes that looked into him. A beggar dog that would not leave. Strange, all of it.

"Guess we'll just let her live," my father said to Fred when Fred showed up one day, carrying his gun. "She's trying hard enough." Fred didn't argue. He'd never wanted to kill the dog in the first place. "I don't know why. I just didn't," he said. "Not that dog."

And White Dog seemed to know the talk of killing was over. She crawled out from the bellied-in place she'd made in the sand under the house—directly under my father's bed—and she crept closer day by day to my father's offerings of food, gravy biscuits being favored. One day, she took the food from my father's hand and then stood still when my father gently scrubbed at her neck. In time, she would rise up, standing on her rear legs, and put her front paws on the front bar of my father's walker, and my father would playfully move about, and White Dog would move with him, like a man-dog dance in an amateur talent contest.

That is the way the two of them lived for years. Special. Attentive. White Dog eating from my father's leftovers. (He purposely over-cooked, though he never admitted doing so. "Table scraps," he said.)

White Dog did not take to anyone else. I was told my sister Lula once touched her, but no one else did that I know of. Whenever any of us went to visit, we could expect to see White Dog skirting the hedges by the tractor barn, body close to the ground, almost invisible, or we could hear her slipping through the shrubbery at the base of the house, scrubbing against the clapboard siding. But we could not call her to us, could not coax her with promises of food. She was there and we knew it. Even when we could not see her, we could sense her.

In 1979, my father was diagnosed with cancer. He would handle himself, being independent, for as long as he could. One day, in early February of 1980, he knew he needed help, and he called one of my sisters to tell her he could no longer make it on his own.

The sisters—there were seven of them, all remarkable—began their swap-off routine of being with him.

And White Dog disappeared. It was on February 4, 1980. On February 5, my father wrote in his journal: *The weatherman says we will have snow before sunup tomorrow. Have just had a phone call from my granddaughter Ann in Knoxville. It is snowing up there. Whitey, my dog, has not been here since yesterday. I hope no harm has come to her.*

On February 6, he wrote: *A beautiful four-inch snow this morning. No school today. Fred and Jimmy did not go to work. Snow is practically gone tonight. Gary has just phoned me. The snow over there is melting. Whitey is still missing. I guess she is gone for no return. She was my best friend. I will miss her.*

My sisters say my father would stand in the yard, leaning on his walker, and call for White Dog for another dance, and when she did not appear, he would search the skies for the circling of buzzards.

"Maybe somebody killed her," we said among ourselves.

"Maybe she just left, like she came."

"He wants us to keep looking."

We never stopped the search, or our wondering. Such a strange relationship the two of them had. Odd. Beautiful. Haunting.

On the night before he died, I learned why. My father said to me, "White Dog was your mother. Come to watch over me until you children took over."

I do not know of such things, but I like the thought of it, and I like the memory of my father's gentleness with White Dog, as though he wanted to embrace a caring he had lost at the death of my mother.

My father died on August 16, 1980.

I do not visit the home place or the cemetery where my parents are buried without looking for the paw prints of White Dog.

I'm sure they're there, somewhere. My father would not have lied to me.

<><><><><><><><><><><><><><><><><><><><><><><><><><><><><><><><>

From *Special Kay: The Wisdom of Terry Kay* (Athens, GA: Hill Street Press, 2000).

Revised, May 5, 2020

"The Strange Dance of the White Dog" is the original story that inspired Terry Kay's Southern classic, *To Dance with the White Dog*. First published in *Atlanta Weekly*, the Sunday magazine section of *The Atlanta Journal-Constitution*, it was later reprinted in *Special Kay*, a collection of essays covering Kay's early career.

The year 2020 marks the 30th anniversary of the publication of *To Dance with the White Dog*, an international bestseller praised by such notables as Archbishop Desmond Tutu and the late Paul Harvey. It was released as a Hallmark Hall of Fame movie in 1993, starring Jessica Tandy and Hume Cronyn and attracting a reported audience of 33 million viewers.

JANISSE RAY

Ephemerals

MY KID CAME HOME ONE THURSDAY AFTERNOON MID-March and said school would be closed for two weeks. The administration called it a "prophylactic" measure, although she didn't know that word.

The world coughed to a stop. Meanwhile, the news sped up, and in three or four days, the coronavirus outbreak was named a pandemic.

I thought I was better prepared than most.

COLLEGE HAD MADE an environmentalist out of me. I understood collapse. We humans needed to live sustainably, or we were going to destroy ourselves and everything we loved. I tacked toward survival.

That was why I lived on a farm, in an old house surrounded by gardens, pasture, and woods. I kept chickens, cows, goats, hogs. My husband and I worked from home, and when office hours were done, we gardened, harvested, made things, fixed things.

We already practiced social distancing, but not because we were hermitic or asocial. We already strung together days where we did not leave the place.

ON THE FARM, mornings were soft, green, and flowery. Coral honeysuckle poured out blooms up a heart pine snag. A buckeye by the mailbox bloomed; the first hummingbird appeared. Grancy Greybeard made its own little cloud. Pecans leafed out.

The only traffic was the migrants coming through, singing in the trees.

I THOUGHT THE lockdown was premature. I thought surely it was a conspiracy. I'd never seen anything like it. Still, I flipped through my calendar, deleting events.

Daily, the numbers of dead grew—800 in one day in Italy. An infectious disease expert predicted that 100,000 Americans would die. At that point, there were 500 cases in Georgia, 20 dead.

WE DID NOT mow the yard, trying to wait as long as possible, and it became a wildflower garden, a sea of tiny spring ephemerals. If UPS delivered a package, I would wade out to the road through a delicate meadow of yellow clovers, dandelions, toadflax, cranesbill, henbit, and sheep sorrel. Sometimes I left the package in the grass. Once, I waited until the driver drove away to take off my shirt. I needed something to protect my hands when I picked up the box.

COWS CONTINUED TO graze, chickens to lay eggs, and ewes to lamb.

I STUDIED THE seedheads of dandelions. The virus had modeled itself after them, a globe made of spikes. In the case of the dandelion, the spikes were soft and drifty. They loosened their hold on the calyx and lofted themselves into the breeze. The orchard, still unmown, was full of them. I told myself to go gather flowers and start dandelion wine. Instead, I watched them turn into seedheads, then scatter in a million directions.

*

THE COCKLEBUR, WITH all its sharp spikes, is a more apt meta-phor. On each coronavirus, spikes are poised to attach to human cell receptors called ACE2s. An average human body has about forty trillion cells, many of them with ACE2 receptors. Proteins on the virus's spikes link to enzymes on our cells, which means they click into place. Cockleburs click into place like this on our clothing, es-pecially wool socks. They burrow in, sharp and painful. This is also how Velcro works.

IN LATE MARCH, one of our horses slipped on a pipe behind the barn, landed on a farm implement, and split open her chest. The vet came despite the pandemic, and she sewed up the horse. I vowed to leave gifts at her office door for the rest of my life.

UPON SEEING A spike, a little voice says, "That looks dangerous." The same is true upon seeing a sharp edge, a heavy object in a precarious lean, or a deep hole. Stop right where you are. Do what you're sup-posed to do. Move the object or fill the hole. Don't make the excuses that invariably follow. You will wish you had listened to that little voice. That voice is god; that voice is you.

A HORSE, HOWEVER, may not be able to hear the voice.

MY HUSBAND HAD retired, so bills got paid. We had an obscene amount of good food. Still, a little voice told me to get ready. We needed disinfectants, more masks, latex gloves, over-the-counter cold medications, the herbs in Stephen Buhner's Coronavirus Protocol.

*

MOST POLLEN HAS the same structure as coronavirus: a bumpy or spiky or rayed globe. It's a familiar motif to humans. After all, it is our sun, our one and only sun, that globe spiking out its gifts of heat and light. If we hold them a certain way, our hands are coronas, too. The coronavirus is a sweetgum ball; it's a grain of ragweed pollen, one of a billion from a single ragweed, drifting along on the wind.

MY DAD, ONE of the most interesting (though spiky) people I've ever known, had died in December, pebble sunk without a ripple. My mother, in the throes of grief and change, was suffering a severe gastrointestinal infection. She called me one evening to tell me she had a fever. "I'm coming," I said. "I'll spend the night." By the next morning, it became clear she needed a hospital.

This was not good. My mother did not have COVID, but she was headed to its epicenter.

We waited until daybreak to leave. The world was quiet, nobody on the road. Soon my mother would be poked with needles, sharp and painful, linked to tubes. I'd be afraid to touch even a doorknob.

All the way to Vidalia, I memorized the landscape, as though I would never see it again—feathers of fog, flushes of red maple, bursts of Carolina jessamine, the way the Georgia sun brings the memory of ocean with it as it comes up in the east. My mother and I spoke quietly, *look at this* and *look at that*.

I felt as though I were driving my mother through the end of the world.

THE HORSE WAS in a fever, leg feverish, stitches busted, her wound oozing and a white foam bubbling out. She had to stay cross-tied. I rigged up a sheet for a bandage, white shawl on a brown horse.

My mother was in a fever.

My brother's wife asked for a divorce.

My child was practicing dystopianism, as teenagers will do.

Ecuador was digging a mass grave. Rhode Island had employed the National Guard to close its border with New York, where the disease was raging. New York City had ordered refrigerated cars for storing the dead. The Navy's medical ship *Mercy* was headed to Los Angeles, where my friend David was working in an ER.

Albany, Georgia, was becoming one of the hardest-hit places in the world.

The word that kept coming to me was *fleeting.* Things are, then they aren't.

ALL SPRING, THE moon and planets made odd and fleeting constellations. The night sky was strewn with the white floating seeds of dandelions. The stars have points, like coronas, which is why the structure of the virus—that crown—is so familiar, so primal. One evening, a crescent moon hung in the western sky, its bow pointed toward Venus. The planet radiated silver light. The next morning, the moon had two planets above it, like eyes, producing a smiley face.

THE SPIKES ON the dandelion lift away, but the center holds.

A STEALTH INVADER threatened to kill any and all of us. The enemy was invisible. It might be living inside me, waiting to crown someone else, using me as a carrier. Mama was out of the hospital, and I wore a mask at all times around her. My husband, Raven, learned that the virus can travel thirteen feet and that it may be tracked in on shoes or in hair: stay home, we were told, wash your hands, don't touch your face, wear a mask.

The center was holding in my household. Survivalists already, we kept the gates closed on our driveway. Outside those gates, the pandemic roared. Raven heard that it might not be as ephemeral as we'd hoped.

My state senator, Jack Hill, died unexpectedly, at his desk, of an apparent heart attack. His assistant checked in with him at five to tell him she was leaving for the day. He was slumped over. He had arrived home from Atlanta a few weeks previously, when the legislature had gotten canceled. Jack was a friend. His death was a blow. His death is a cocklebur, a globe of painful spikes. The loss catches in my clothes and in my hair. I can't get it out.

Later, I heard that his housekeeper tested positive.

JOHN PRINE'S DEATH was a blow, too.

ON APRIL 13, my brother's cell phone pinged the first patient testing positive at Appling Pavilion. That's the nursing facility in my home county. I have a lot of friends who live there. Little spiky globes began to blow like pollen through the Pavilion. Dozens of residents and staff were testing positive. Some were rolling down the hallway into the hospital, into the ICU, onto ventilators. The first patient died. He was a friend of our family. His daughter had to stand outside his window in the middle of the night as he floated away.

ANOTHER SEED SPUN off, then another. It seemed we were in a huge kill-off of our old people. In a year, people would hardly remember who Jack Hill even was.

I had thought I was prepared. But I wasn't. I lit candles for all suffering, a rose quartz in my hand.

The pandemic took away all community and all semblance of community. That was a huge loss, because community is how we survive and thrive.

But that was only one side of an equation.

The pandemic gave, too. In the end, it gave more time to contemplate, to sit with the anxiety of invasion, to be with the inevitability of death, to stop being emotional and start being wise, to be still, to deepen into one's place, to notice beauty, to take a deep breath in the fleeting floatingness and in the floating fleetingness of our lives.

My horse Santara could now move around a bit during the day. Before bed, I would go out and tuck her in. The Big Dipper was above us, and the Little Dipper, along with Orion and dozens of constellations visible or partly visible through the trees. I would go out under a rich canopy of stars and into the pen where I kept Santara, cross-tie her, and put on her fly mask, which I thought would make her less scared by herself at night because it muted sounds and sight. In the dark, I cleaned her wound and changed the bandage. I would spray her with insect repellent and drape a horse blanket over her back.

Every night, her head was lowered. She would turn around like a good dog and bump me with her nose.

Sometimes I rubbed her a little, a massage down the back.

One night, I stood near her and talked. *We won't be remembered,* I said. *You won't because you're just a horse. So many amazing, stunning horses have lived and died, and we know nothing about any of them.*

Because you won't be remembered, you represent all horses that ever lived, breathed, ran, reared, shied, flicked flies, and felt unsayable things. You are all horses.

And if you are all horses, I said, *then I'm all people. I'm a seed in the long march of humanity, endless train of people living, breathing, running, rearing, shying, flicking flies, and feeling unsayable things.*

Underneath the diamond umbrella of night sky floating with seeds and burs, I joined the river that rises from the ground, flows across the land for a while, then disappears underground—and yet keeps flowing. I represent that river. I am all humans. I am all of them. I am the movement.

Goodnight, girl, I said, exactly like millions of other humans who rose and went out into darkness to care for hurt mares or geldings or stallions. *See you in the morning.*

*

THE SPRING OF 2020 will be remembered as the Spring of the Garden. Ours was looking good. I was finally tackling an infestation of nutgrass. For thirty minutes every day, I dug it.

We live on a flightpath into Jacksonville, and no matter the time of day, I was used to looking up into the crosshatches of contrails. Now I would look up at the sky and it would be blue as a bunting, clouds sailing through it like a regatta. I looked up into the clear, blue, flawless skies of my youth.

Death was all around me. Every human on the globe was in danger. The enemy moved invisibly in my midst. I held my breath as it floated toward me. I did not need one of death's spikes to click into place.

Yet I listened to the birds. I could hear the earth in a way I had seldom heard it. The noises of enterprise had quieted.

Coronavirus had done something that all the environmentalists in the world had failed to do. It had proven that we humans do want to save ourselves.

I WANT TO save myself. I want to save the world. I always have. In the time I have, I want to help the world be a better place. What I'm afraid of is suffering.

RAVEN WENT INTO a dollar store for reading glasses and suddenly felt flush on the way out. My friend Holly got symptoms, went to a testing site, an hour round-trip, and was told the wait was three hours and they wouldn't be able to get to her that day. The next day, she drove back and the site was closed. Appling County's positive test results were approaching 300. Then 400. Then 500. Deaths were at fourteen. Then fifteen.

"The Shuman boys have it" and "It got spread at Watermelon Creek Church by a wedding" and "Dale's daughter tested positive but she's asymptomatic" and "He's in quarantine."

My neighbor began to have symptoms. My first cousin tested positive, remained asymptomatic. My mother's telehealth nurse knew a couple in Savannah with two young children. Both the husband and wife were in the hospital for COVID. The husband had kidney damage and had to go on dialysis.

THE NATURE OF nutgrass is viral. From soft dirt, I lift it out in networks. I dig one, follow a leader to another, and dig it, setting off a chain reaction as I excise them. One nutgrass is connected to many. From each nut, the grass sends leaders off in many directions, establishing a fort at the end of each, which in turn sends grass stalks up and leaders out. It's a crazy network. It's stars in the sky, connected by thin lines. Digging nutgrass is contact tracing.

COVID IS A weed—like dandelion, like nutgrass, like cockleburs. It is an imperialist. It colonizes. It wants territory. It floats in, plants a flag, and flies on.

By June, it was overtaking Georgia. It would pass or not pass, at its own pace. Our lives would return to normal or transform completely.

THE CENTER THAT holds is our hearts, which are made for love. Our hearts are seeds in a flowing river of seeds. We are the movement of love.

MAY GOODNESS AND love radiate out toward all others. May my consciousness join all the consciousnesses of the universe. Let my sight broaden beyond the trees, into infinity. Let me sit with the peace flooding my body. Let me hover between effort and effortlessness. Life is not about being perfect. Life is about joy. Let me be in the moment I have. May we all be at peace, free of suffering.

*

GOODNESS AND LOVE are viral, too. They want to colonize. They want to attach their spikes to our cells and make their way through every organ of our bodies. May we all be thus infected.

MARGARET ELIZABETH BROOK

We Aren't Going Out Now

Diversion denied,
That's the way I describe
These days now.
Shut inside the world we've assembled
And yet now disassembled,
Our focus is changed.
Our self-perception now humbled,
We see where we've stumbled
As we get a closer view,
A clearer view,
Of what we can't escape
Here, in quarantine.
All the kindness we could have shared,
Thoughtful gestures overlooked,
Phone calls unreturned,
Put off for another day
While we chased what we'd long forgotten.
Only now we see
How none of that really mattered
When we were so scattered
And free, free to be
Caught in a whirlwind, when no
Breeze stirred a tree.
And so I ask myself this question:

When the doors open wide and safety slips inside,
Will I do better
When I'm unfettered,
And stop and mend each broken heart?

RICKI CARDENAS

Corona Care Package

M Y VIDEO DOORBELL APP GOES OFF—CHIMES *JANG-A-langing* through my townhouse—waking Boomer from a hard sleep.

"*Bowwww!*" He's a sixty-five-pound tangle of legs and ears on his way to the front door.

"Quiet, boy. It's okay!" I dab at the coffee I, of course, spilled all down my front.

But the spike in my blood pressure says otherwise—I've been eyeball-deep in spreadsheets and e-mails all morning without the disturbance of so much as a bird chirping.

I set my laptop on the ottoman with a *plop* and take a few deep breaths.

"I'm sure it's just…" But even as I go through my mental list of Amazon items slated to come this week, I come up with nothing.

Chewing one corner of my lip, I scroll to the live feed of the doorbell cam on my phone to see who it could be.

But it's no one. And, when I rewind the video, there's nothing to show why it went off in the first place.

"Either a glitch or the wind," I say in reassuring tones, but Boomer's forehead wrinkles still approach the ceiling.

I'm already up, so I humor the poor boy and tiptoe my way to the door.

Peek through my blinds… and stop in my tracks.

There it is.

Not a cardboard box of wonder with a little arrow smile. Not a white, padded envelope containing my favorite discontinued moisturizer.

Not even the ninety-six pack of Victor Allen coffee pods that arrives faithfully every two months.

I step back, the slats of the blinds snapping shut with a *thwap*, and my heart pounds.

Relax, Pru.

Boomer looks up at me, watery eyes full of concern, and I lay a hand on his lumpy head. He lowers his haunches and flops onto his behind—and it's then that I open the door with all the care of a bomb squad technician.

The sweet smell of the crepe myrtle out front is a hypnotist's watch, and the humidity laps at my bare arms. The two sensations pull me closer to the threshold. Closer to the item highlighted in an otherworldly glow from the beam of the mid-afternoon sun.

A marshmallow heap, right there on my welcome mat, gleaming up at me in all its glory:

A single roll of toilet paper.

"MY GOD, PRU." Yazzi gapes from her spot on the phone screen, her tone operatic. "You didn't bring it in, did you?"

Blotches of concern burn in her cheeks, the judgment in her question pulsing through the air and reaching me all the way from Detroit.

I avert my stare to my muted TV. To the pan of mac 'n' cheese I left on the stove. Back to her image on my phone.

"I mean—not yet..."

"You should never have moved there, Pru. Job schmob." She's pacing now. "What kind of psycho leaves a roll of toilet paper at your front door?"

I stretch out on my chaise and sigh. "It's a question I've asked myself all afternoon, but I've come up with zilch. I don't know anyone down here yet. Maybe someone left it by mistake. Maybe it was a plumber. A grocery delivery person—"

"A serial killer."

Baby Sammy cries on her end, and I lift an eyebrow. "What's he going to do, strangle me to death with TP? I think I could survive that, Yaz."

She ignores me, and the screen goes all shaky as she makes her way to the baby swing. "Was there anything else? A note? A severed head?"

I laugh. "Nope—just the Cottonelle... Damn, and that's my favorite, too. I haven't been able to get anything but the one-ply Walmart brand in weeks."

"I know—you told me."

"I did?" I lose myself in a reverie of when that could have been.

"Yes, during one of your walks. Your whole neighborhood probably knows." She clucks her tongue. "So, how are you going to solve the mystery of Poo Radley?"

I choke on my last swig of coffee and launch into a coughing fit I wouldn't dare allow in the vicinity of people, for fear of being labeled as having the 'Rona.

Once the offending liquid has gone down the correct pipe, I wheeze back at my friend, "I don't have a fricking clue. It does remind me, however, that I need to go to the store."

I screech into a spot, leaving five empty ones between my Malibu and a minivan with one of those stick-figure families affixed to the left side of the back window.

There's a pang in my chest at the two stick girls and one stick boy.

The image must trigger my glutton-for-punishment hormone, because I get the sudden urge to call my mom so she can ask if I've met anyone husband-worthy yet.

I scan the parking lot as I cross it—no one else near—so I yank my Georgia Tech ball cap down over my eyes, pull my mask into place, and it's like I'm the Invisible Man.

I don't know why, but I hold my breath as I enter Publix.

Every person is an obstacle. Every way I go is wrong. I'm exactly the opposite of the green arrows and red X's denoting the flow of the foot traffic. Totally out of sync with the rest of the world.

You should never have moved there, Pru.

Yazzi's words echo between my ears as I zig and zag, narrowly avoiding human landmines.

Down Aisle 9, I lock gazes with a squat woman who snatches the last bag of rice and hunches over it like she's Gollum.

Rice isn't on my list anyway, but I know how she feels. Like everyone's a superspreader. Like everyone's an enemy, out to take your "precious." In the interest of camaraderie—of humanity—I offer her a smile. *Get your rice, lady. No one's mad at you.*

Beads of sweat stipple the lower half of my face, and I wonder what this woman thinks my expression is supposed to communicate.

That you're a psycho killer, Yazzi'd probably say.

And Yaz probably wouldn't be that far off, the way Lady Gollum cuts her stare back to her prize and shrinks further into herself without returning the gesture.

I exhale all the optimism I've mustered—thank God I remembered to chew gum this time—and press my lips into a small frown. Not that anyone can see it, anyway.

I skirt my way past Sméagol, past the cans of reject vegetables no one buys, and head down the next aisle.

It's barren of everything I actually need—unless I want the Publix version of brittle butt paper (I don't)—and I grin at the thought of the gem still waiting for me at my door.

I SPEND THE rest of the afternoon eating DoorDash leftovers and finishing up my task list for work, but I'm distracted by my mysterious gift.

My mind races as I run on my treadmill. Spins as I fold laundry.

And then? A snap of my fingers.

"I've got it," I tell Yazzi. "I bet everyone got something. Like it's some neighborly coronavirus care package initiative."

"Very logical, Mr. Spock." She throws up a Live Long and Prosper hand sign, and we both chuckle.

After our evening catch-up, I take to my neighborhood community Facebook page to confirm my theory and see if I missed a "coming together" post.

But it's mainly complaints. No parking on the street *this*. Trashcans left out too long *that*. Interspersed with *I'm selling my lumpy, tired couch for $120, OBO* and *Does anyone have any recommendations on an inexpensive carpet cleaner?*

I squish my face and wiggle my fingers over the keyboard.

Dear Neighbors,

I'm newish here, so I wanted to say hello and also ask if anyone knows who the Toilet Paper Fairy is? I want to thank the Good Samaritan for this Pay-It-Forward gesture—and can someone tell me how I can participate?

There's a flutter behind my ribs as the post goes live—and it's an uneventful hour, as I watch how many folks have viewed it but not commented.

I give up around thirty-seven.

It's just about sunset, and the humidity is—well—not as little as it would be back in Detroit, but much more tolerable than it was the rest of the day. I get Boomer leashed up, I throw on some yoga pants, and we set out on our nightly stroll through the townhouse community.

The neighborhood is abuzz with activity as we make our way through the streets.

I guess, if I want to make friends, this is the best time of day to see people out and about.

Two Doors Down Guy is washing his Camaro as I close my garage. His dark eyes flash at me from underneath a backward baseball cap as he bops along to whatever he's listening to with his wireless earbuds.

I offer a nod and wish I'd put on some makeup—*Do I even remember how at this point?*

Very Pregnant Chick waddles along after her toddler on a tricycle. She's not very friendly—she never is—even though her boy always points and says, "Look, Momma—dog!" and grins at Boomer. She's acted like we both carry the plague even before COVID, so why would now be any different?

Old Man and Old Lab both lumber by without a second glance, even when Boomer gives a playful bark. I decide it's probably less out of rudeness and more out of the fact that neither of them can probably hear very well.

The only two masks I see are worn by the couple who jog up and down the big hill. Everyone else is at a safe distance, and so it feels more normal than the grocery store. And nice, to see other humans not on a phone or laptop screen.

But it still feels different.

Very few people actually smile.

A trio of tween girls writing their names in sidewalk chalk are all giggles as Boomer and I make the turn down Cavender Way.

I think of Yazzi and me doing the same thing at their age, and I get lost in the same conversations. Although, instead of Michael, Eddie, or Robert, they're buzzing about Jackson, Taylor, and Mason. Instead of the pictures they have in their lockers, they talk about their backgrounds on Zoom. Catching glimpses of one of the boys' bedroom walls.

My heart aches for Yazzi, for my mom, for home. And I wonder just where the last twenty-five years have gone.

"Can we pet your dog?" The one with pom-pom pigtails yanks me out of yesteryear.

I chuckle, a hand to my chest. "Sure, you can pet Boomer. As long as it's okay with your parents…"

The redhead tosses a hand. "They let us pet every dog."

A smile takes over my face, and I glance around the street, looking for other signs of life as Boomer lays on the lover boy act. The girls coo over him, and my gaze lands on the open garage across the street.

Like a beacon, a fortress of toilet paper packages—all Cottonelle—lines the whole back wall.

I snap to attention. "Do you know who lives there?" I ask the girls, who sit cross-legged on the pavement and rub Boomer's tummy.

The tallest girl crosses her spindly arms over her polka-dot tank top. "Ebenezer Scrooge's wife."

A laugh popcorns out of me. "So not the Toilet Paper Fairy, then?"

The girls give me grimaces with varying degrees of *Wha-huh?*

"That old lady bought up all the toilet paper at Costco the first week of quarantine," the first one says, "and she's not sharing with anybody."

I crane my neck to see what else Mrs. Scrooge has in her arsenal. All I can make out is cans of Maxwell House stacked floor-to-ceiling and rows of unopened antibacterial handwipes.

Boomer and I say our goodbyes, but I can't help feeling low as we stroll past the gazebo. The trees turn to silhouettes against a purpling sky, and I think of the neighborly initiative.

Where are those friendly people now?

My phone weighs down my pocket, so I pull it out to check my post, and—lo and behold—there's a response.

It's from someone named Alex Santos, who of course doesn't have a photo of himself as his profile picture. Just an Air Force logo.

It was just for you, but I'm game to start something like that. What a fun way to bring us all together!

My blood surges through my veins, and I'm suddenly on high alert.

My breaths are shallow, and, for a moment, I worry someone will think I'm displaying another COVID symptom.

I lean over my knees and look back at the message.

This time, the winky face posted with the message calms me down. I'm able to slow my pulse to human levels again—and I'm even able to send Yazzi a screenshot of the response so she can start her obligatory Facebook investigation of Alex Santos.

I'm chuckling at the thought of her, frantic at the keyboard—that is, until I arrive in front of my townhouse.

It's there that I stop dead at the now THREE objects in front of my garage door.

I creep closer and discover it's a bottle of Corona Extra, a coffee pod, and another roll of Cottonelle—this time, with a Post-it note on top of it.

I thought I'd ask you while I'm on a roll… (ba-dum-bum!)
Do you want to grab a socially distant drink sometime?

I gasp, hands climbing to my cheeks, and Boomer's leash slips from my fingers.

He takes off down the street, and there's no time to think. I'm running—legs ignited with adrenaline—my thighs, my calves, burning out.

A luge-speed version of the leisurely walk we've just taken blurs past, but I lose Boomer on the second turn.

I'm yelling—spewing spit and sweat as I desperately call his name.

Panic welling in my eyes, I'm defeated when I make the final turn toward home again; but, there that goober is, sitting in my driveway, banging his tail against the pavement.

He's beaming up at Two Doors Down Guy, who's crouched beside him in basketball shorts and a tee.

"Oh, thank you!" I sprint the rest of the way there, my body giving out as soon as I reach the two of them. I grasp for Boomer's leash, and he's all licks and flops, as though I haven't been with him all day.

Two Doors Down Guy stands up and straightens his shirt, the bottom half of an eagle tattoo on his bicep peeking out from one sleeve.

His dark eyes shine with concern while I catch my breath. "I'm really sorry," he says, his voice gentle. "That was totally my fault. I'm Alex, by the way." He holds out a hand, then yanks it back like he's just touched fire. "Oh, I'm sorry. We're probably not supposed to—" He shakes his head and scratches at the back of his neck. "I hate this."

My mouth hangs open, but I can't form words.

"I didn't mean to freak you out," he says, indicating the beer, coffee, and TP. "I just wanted to meet you. Pretty stupid, I know."

He twists his sweet face into a frown and scoops up the offending items, each one threatening to jump right out of his grasp, then heads in the direction of his place.

I'm blinking at the back of him, finally able to swallow, finally able to breathe again—and then:

"Alex—wait." I will the quiver out of my voice. "How about now?"

He jerks to a halt and does a sheepish about-face.

"You asked if I wanted to have a drink sometime…" I continue, holding Boomer's leash steady.

As Alex meets my gaze, his whole posture relaxes. He takes a small step forward, the hint of a dimple deepening in the streetlight that just clicked on above him.

Fireflies twinkle all around in the darkening sky, and I too slide on a smile.

"Where the heck are you going with my beer?"

DEVI S. LASKAR

Excerpt from
Salt of the Continents

1 month before

TIRED OF THE ONSLAUGHT OF YOUR HOMECOOKED MEALS and the dominance of chickpea coconut curry and daal and, alternatively, pasta with tomato and garlic and basil, M— calls around and finds the KFC on Johnson Ferry Road still open. "Talked to Josh," he says, brown eyes alight. "Maybe we can have one night of something greasy and unhealthy."

Josh is the KFC manager, a classmate from your months at the local high school and your husband's friend from little league eons ago. M— says Josh bought everyone paper masks and latex gloves from the dollar store before they ran out and is keeping the franchise open. "Totally safe," he says, rubbing his hands together. Eleven to six, Monday through Sunday.

M— has a conference call on a new business venture, so you volunteer to drive.

You arrive when the line has snaked past the drugstore that was boarded up after a run on the toilet paper and paper towels. Frustrated consumers had thrown bricks and stones through the plate glass to express their anger; shards of glass still glitter everywhere.

By the time you reach the front, all the buckets of crisply fried chicken are gone, and all of the sides, Styrofoam bowls of green beans and mashed potatoes with brown gravy glistening on top. Just a few lonely biscuits on the warming tray under a lamp and masked employees shrugging as they give muffled apologies.

Josh, your once-upon-a-time classmate, tells you to come back first thing in the morning, that he'll save you some. Regret swims in his crystal-blue eyes.

"Give M— my best," he says, pressing a biscuit wrapped in paper into your hand.

You come home and drop the biscuit onto the table, meaning to throw some jam onto it and make a peace offering. But Mo jumps up and noses past the paper wrapping, gobbling half before you can snatch it away. "That's all there was," you say when M— comes out of the study.

M— looks you over, from your roots that need touching up down to your ancient *Bata* sandals from Kolkata, the Havana-red polish on your toes chipped and in need of professional care.

His smile is understanding, kind even.

But he slams the door to his office hard and doesn't come out for the rest of the night.

2

This morning, M— was gone by the time you woke up, the sun shining like a bald-faced lie through the open window, Mo snoring beside you.

3

The woman says, "...*ever more bitter with the salt of the continents.*"

*

YOUR FEET DANGLE off the side of the couch as you wait. You're hungry, but you don't want to eat alone. M— is late, which is not new, but surprisingly, he hasn't even called to check in. You can't find Mo. He must be out exploring again in the woods by the chain-link fence in the back, or he's found a fuzzy sock and is cheerfully shredding it in some corner. You're reading an article—rather you're listening to an audio version of it—on Rachel Carson and how, as a trained marine biologist, she came to write her seminal book about the pesticide poisoning of nature: *Silent Spring*.

The telephone rings. The woman on the other end calls from a university you once gave money to, for a former friend's PhD project. "We'd love to have you contribute at the leadership level this year," she says as voices chirp and telephones trill in the distance.

Sounds expensive. "I can't help you today," you say as softly as you can, because you're the type of girl who hates to disappoint anyone. Even a stranger. "But try me again."

"I understand," she says, though her young voice is now clipped. She doesn't sound like she does understand. She doesn't know you; she doesn't know how unevenly your income is distributed among the mountain range of bills and debts and family obligations.

You say goodbye and hang up.

"Mo," you call out. "Come here, boy."

Silence.

Not like your brown-eyed dachshund mix. He usually stays close by, especially at dinnertime. You found him a few months ago at the humane shelter outside Norcross, during its young-adult rescue day. He was eating a doggie biscuit. "You're just a cookie monster, aren't you?" said the old lady who was feeding him as he snuggled into her lap, his teeth firmly on the treat.

You laughed. You were going to call him Cookie but then learned he was a boy. A boy who needed to be neutered.

So Monster became Mo, and together, you went home.

Within a day, the governor imposed shelter-in-place orders and you were stuck at home. Indefinitely.

THE NARRATION OF Carson's profile continues: *"...some evil spell had fallen on the community..."*

THE UNIVERSITY LADY calls back a minute later. "Please," she says, introducing herself as Rachel, a scholarship student who spends her evenings on the telephone as part of her work-study exchange. "I have to meet my quota tonight."

Yet another Rachel.

Your stepdaughter with the same name walks into the house; the wind ushers her in. You watch her struggle to shut the door. Your almost-child on the verge of college and flight. You say to the Rachel-named voice on the phone: "Please try me again at another time." You used to work at a call center. You may yet return to that life-depleting job. You hate to be rude.

Your almost-daughter asks, "Who was that?" as she turns away from you and goes down the hall and into her room.

"A solicitor," you say.

But she's shut the door and turned on her radio. All that's left of this interchange is the faint scent of her perfume and the remnants of the cool breeze.

You shiver. "Mo," you say to the empty room. "Where are you, boy?"

Your almost-daughter turns up the volume.

"...COLOR THAT FLAMED and flickered across a backdrop..."

*

YOUR STOMACH RUMBLES like distant thunder.

Several minutes later, the telephone rings again. The woman from the university you never attended is calling back.

"I think you misunderstood me," she says when you answer and say hello. "You don't have to give the same amount as last year."

You count to ten, first in Bengali and then in French, in your head. You pray she will get the hint from your silence. Then: "For the third time, I can't help you today."

A garbled noise. Is she crying? Clearing her throat? Finally: "Don't you care about your university? You were once so generous."

You try not to laugh. "I never went there," you say. "I only gave to support my friend." You can't help but chuckle. "Her name is Rachel, too."

"Oh," this Rachel says. "Well, I'm sure she will appreciate your continued support."

You shake your head. But she can't see you. "She's dead, so she doesn't really care anymore."

And this is true and not true. Rachel Clarke's death, you mean. She may still be alive. But she is dead to you, this friend you once helped.

The Rachel on the telephone gasps.

You say goodbye and hang up, then press the pause button on the article.

You walk down the hallway, tap on the teenager's door. "May I come in?"

Your almost-daughter Rachel's voice is muffled but exasperated. "If you must."

You open the door, and Rachel's room is a landfill in progress: on the ground, piles of discarded clothes, the makings of a collage next to glue sticks, scissors, nail polish remover, tubes of foundation, several pairs of shoes, though the rules are to leave all footwear in the cubbies by the front door. You try not to sigh or say anything; your relationship is tenuous most days, as she toggles between two households and two sets of expectations. You remain, relatively speaking, a new mother, but the only true parent this Rachel has ever had. "I can't find Mo," you say. "Have you seen him?" You lock eyes with her and are reminded of M—. He wasn't pleased at first, when Mo came home with you. *You travel too much. What am I going to do with a dog when you're gone?* You handed him Mo's leash and said, *Walk.*

Mo is a worshipper of this Rachel. When she is at your house, he is a follower, guarding her with precious intensity—she is his god, and he listens to everything she says. You look around, half-expecting Mo to be hiding in a soft pile of Rachel's denim.

Rachel hesitates. "I saw him a couple of hours ago."

You raise your eyebrows. "And?"

She smiles a little. "I know I'm not supposed to, but he looked hungry."

You try to shrug off your irritation, which swirls in the air between you like dust. "What did you give him?"

Rachel opens her phone and shows off photos she's posted on social media: Mo at the table, eating from her hand; Mo sitting on his back legs, eating chicken and rice from a stainless-steel bowl; Rachel posing Mo in a birthday cone hat and sunglasses for a photo shoot.

"Really cute," you say, touching Mo's face on the screen for a moment. "Did you let him outside?"

She nods. "I... opened the door." She throws her cell onto the beanbag across the room, and it lands with an emphatic thud. "He really wanted to go... out."

You turn to leave. "I can make breakfast for dinner, if you want."

She doesn't reply.

You look back; her eyes are hollow.

"I'm not hungry," she says. "I might go back to Mom's."

You work hard to keep your face expressionless. Rachel does not respond well to confrontation, and her parents, M— and that shrew of an ex-wife, ride her frequently and with the same frequency; that is to say, they are thoughtless and forgetful. "Suit yourself."

*

You crack a few eggs into the hot pan already sizzling with butter. You start to make a fried egg, but your hand slips and the spatula nicks the center and yolk spills. "Shit." You take the tip of the spatula and zigzag through the clear whites and other yolk and make an ugly, uneven scramble.

You find the last of the bread in the fridge and pop the two ends into the toaster. You look around and sigh, another exhausting trip to the grocery store looming on the horizon as you notice you are out of apples and oranges and there is a lone banana hanging like a crescent moon from a metal tabletop tree. You hear Rachel come out of her room, the hinges squeaking in protest. "Bye," she calls out, and then the front door slams shut. She revs her engine and pulls away.

You go to throw away the eggshells and notice the KFC wrapper balled up and resting in the recycling can, next to the organic waste. You tried yesterday to make M— happy. You sigh and resolve to apologize for allowing Mo to eat most of the biscuit.

In between bites of broken eggs, you try calling M— again. The phone rings a couple of times and then his voice comes on, modulated and warm, repeating his telephone number but not giving his name, instructing the caller to leave a message and saying that he'll return the call. You hang up before the call switches over to voicemail. You save a bit of egg and a bite of your buttered toast in a bowl, for Mo. You open the door to the backyard and call Mo's name. A crow caws in reply.

After you load the dishwasher, you try M— again.

This time you wait for the beep. "Are you out foraging for grease?" you ask into the receiver. "Are you still mad?" You have other questions, but you hope these two are enough to make him smile and call you back. You hang up and check the wall calendar. Two days until your second wedding anniversary. You don't know what the appropriate gifts are under normal circumstances, and you don't care. You intend to bake bread in this time of epidemic. Fancy hamburger buns, in fact.

If it's grease he wants, then so be it. Cheeseburgers on the grill to go with the beer chilling in the fridge.

◇◇

Note: Quotations from Ms. Carson were taken from Jill Lepore, "The Right Way to Remember Rachel Carson," *The New Yorker*, March 26, 2018.

www.newyorker.com/magazine/2018/03/26/
the-right-way-to-remember-rachel-carson/amp

GINGER EAGER

The Realm of the Non-Living Mothers

"THINK OF YOUR MOTHER," VENERABLE KHADRO INSTRUCTS from my computer screen. According to the schedule, she's supposed to be teaching rather than leading a meditation, but this isn't the first time lines have blurred during the virtual retreat.

I soften my gaze, and in my mind's eye, my mother appears. She's at the stove. Her hair is clipped in short '80s wings, and her lips are the brick-red color that was her signature until Revlon discontinued it. I'm lying in front of the refrigerator, reciting the losses and victories of my fourth-grade day. She nudges me with her foot. "Get out from in front of there." I squirm away just enough for her to crack the fridge door and grab what she needs. Then I roll back to the spot I've warmed on the linoleum.

Venerable Khadro adjusts her robes. "This image of your mother isn't your mother. You may have feelings about this image similar to the feelings you have for your mother, but this image isn't your living mother."

No, of course not. My living mother has returned to the hospital to be with my father, who, as of today, I'm pleased to report, is himself still among the living.

Two hours ago, I sat with my mother at her kitchen table. (Same kitchen, different table.) No masks. This was the first time

I'd been inside her house since March. She ate the baked chicken and mashed potatoes I'd brought. Her hair hadn't been colored in months, and for the first time, I could see her graying pattern, silver on the sides and dark at the crown. *Is that how my hair will gray?* I wondered, and I heard my dead grandmother chuckle and say, *If you're lucky!*

My mother's mother made this joke once while she was living, and since the quarantine began, she's taken to making it often in my head.

Am I going to get fat after menopause?

If you're lucky!

Am I going to get glaucoma in my seventies?

If you're lucky!

Venerable Khadro's voice is gentle. "This image of your mother is a mental phenomenon, arising and passing. Think of the mind not as an organ sitting inside of you but as a stream, a flowing river, a continuum, changing every nanosecond."

The internet glitches, and Venerable Khadro freezes for a moment. I signed up for this retreat only a few days ago. I can do it because it's virtual, and my job is virtual, too. From the spare bedroom of my house in Decatur, Georgia, I watch Sravasti Abbey's Vimeo channel. The Abbey is on the other side of the continent, in Washington State. The time difference leaves me early mornings to grade papers, answer emails, meet students' needs. The nuns of Sravasti Abbey want me to honor this retreat as though I were there, and I do from 8:30 a.m. to 9:00 p.m. Or part of me does, anyway. Enough of me, maybe. All of me that I can give. Even on the days I cook for my mother, I still spend hours in front of a piano bench I picked up from the roadside and repurposed as an altar. The rocks and feathers are pushed to the side to make space for my laptop.

Venerable Khadro says, "There are many types of mental phenomena. We'll discuss them later in the retreat."

But I want her to discuss this now. Mental images and memories—are these different? And what about feelings? Where do they come from?

I've missed whatever it is that Venerable just said.

I feel I am not paying attention.

In the past, when my father was hospitalized, my brother and I flanked his hospital bed. This time, only our mother can be with him. We last saw him in the emergency room, waiting to begin blood transfusions. I imagine him as he was then: breath shallow, so weak he needed to rest between sentences, still cracking jokes. I imagine my mother there with him, pulling the blue curtain for privacy. It's all quite soothing until I'm jolted by fact: Dad's no longer in the ER. I conjure a proper hospital room: bathroom, television, green vinyl chair, a window with a view of Peachtree Street. There's The Shakespeare Tavern.

Not long before the quarantine began, my husband and I saw *Julius Caesar* at the Tavern. For seventeen years, each time my father was released from the heart ward at Crawford Long, one of us would say, "We should see a play sometime." This sentence was just marriage-code for "Whew, everything's okay again," until our son left for college and we decided to discover Atlanta anew. During *Julius Caesar*, I embarrassed myself by sobbing. "Four hundred years and people still love Shakespeare," I said. "Imagine." The image I hold from that moment is of my empty cider glass.

Venerable Khadro won't stop talking. "Some of us still have living mothers," she says, "but they're not here with us in this room."

"I'm not in the room with you, either," I snap. Neither are the other fifty-eight participants on this Vimeo call. Can't I be left, for just a moment, with my mother in her brick-red lipstick?

Venerable motions into the distance with a thin hand. "The living mothers are out there somewhere."

Mother, father, grandmother. Flesh, and flesh, and spirit. Alive, and fighting for life, and no longer living. I'm alive now, but I'll also know fighting for life and no longer living. My mother, father, and grandmother are at once present with me and absent from me. I too am present and absent, watching this livestream in my spare bedroom and contemplating the nature of mind.

Many of the details, I've gotten wrong. This time, my father isn't in the heart ward at Crawford Long, but at Gwinnett Medical. I've never been inside a room at Gwinnett Medical. And even though I've been in many rooms at Crawford Long, I've crafted a make-believe view. The heart ward doesn't look out onto Peachtree Street. This image of The Shakespeare Tavern must be from somewhere else in the hospital; the walkway, perhaps. My mind has cobbled places together in an effort to know where my father is, and it has cobbled experiences together in an effort to understand what he's facing. But what he faces this time isn't related to his heart. His COVID test was negative, too. At this moment, the "why" of his situation isn't the one I would expect from his past or the one I would expect from the present. The "why" of now is still being sought.

My mother communicates with my brother and me mostly through texts. She sends what details she has and we ask questions, back and forth, back and forth, until we run out of words and send little red and purple hearts instead, little yellow prayer hands.

Venerable Khadro is taking questions.

Where are the non-living mothers? I type into the comment box. This would be a good thing to know. The non-living mothers are surely in the same place as other non-living beings. Stalled in an inter-realm traffic jam, detained in a sprawling border camp. The global death toll is over half a million. I'm terrified of losing my father in this exodus. I hit enter, but my question doesn't post. I'm not logged in. All this time, I've been watching as a guest.

There must be some other way to submit comments.

If you're lucky! my grandmother says.

WILLIAM WALSH

Hey! Get Off My Lawn: Thoughts During the Quarantine

YES, TO HAVE SO MUCH TIME—TO DO NOTHING OR everything? It's a luxury many people have dreamt about, including myself; however, it is, as I have discovered, a burden. My house has never been cleaner. Despite working from home with so much time on my hands, busy with my administrative duties from the university and teaching, and yet, because I am home all the time, I feel as though I am unemployed. For the first month, there seemed to be an endless amount of work, because students do not start their day at 6:00 a.m. each morning, as I do. They stagger in from noon to three o'clock or closer to midnight. There is an overwhelming sense of failure if I am not there for them, ready at the helm to teach at all hours, to answer questions, reply to emails. Being stuck in my house has led to many revelations. Among them, the most important being: I have decided, *I will never retire*. I may not always teach college, but I will have a job doing something. Retirement appears to be overrated, and I never want to be stuck at home again.

Just write novels, a friend said. I wish. Even though I am finishing two new novels, *Haircuts for the Dead* and *The Boomerang Mattress*, it's not so easy. When I have all the time in the world, I get very little accomplished. When I am pressed, I find pockets of time to squirrel away and edit or write a new page. I get things done, but I now understand that I need the distraction of work and being away from my writing to feel compelled to write. And, most importantly, to think. My deep contemplative thinking occurs away from my house. Not all of it, but I love driving to work and sorting out writing issues and life's problems in the car. I think back to Faulkner living and writing at Rowan Oak, Frost's Stone House in Vermont, Flannery O'Connor's Andalusia, Hemingway in Key West, and Thoreau's Walden Pond. My basement has as much personality as a DMV teller booth. This is the place I type but not where I create and dream and imagine the world as I want it to be for my poems or the characters in a novel, or for myself. It is really nothing more than the place I sit to type, as I am doing at this very moment. Few dreams have ever been created in my basement. It is, as I eye the furniture and books, utilitarian at best. I do my greatest thinking in the car or when riding my bike or walking the dogs, not in a La-Z-Boy in my office. However, I had a revelation.

What is my life like during a pandemic? I get up, I make coffee, and I'm in my chair by six. I've stretched that now to seven. Oddly, I watch less television than before, only when I stop for lunch or dinner or *Jeopardy!*, which is a nightly family ritual. The boys are back from college, which I know they hate because there are rules they have to live by. There are no jobs, so they are finding makeshift work here and there and trying to stay busy. My daughter and I have played a lot of boardgames: *Risk, Monopoly, Connect Four, Battleship, Sorry,* and *Clue.* The jigsaw puzzle we put together had twelve pieces missing.

I've made sure my mother is doing fine and has what she needs. When I asked if it's okay to visit, she said, "You're going to die from something." She's eighty-four and going strong, but she has taken a cavalier attitude toward the pandemic and the rules and regulations that have her confined to home. I know that is irritating. Age has not slowed her down, and won't. She is a racehorse waiting each morning for the gate to swing open.

I'm taking the dogs for more walks, more late-night car rides with the kids. I'm playing more golf because it is open-air. I played tennis until the courts were shut down. I read *A Prayer for Owen Meany* and a biography of C.S. Lewis. I wrote a book review of *Weathering* by David Havird and *Obscura* by Frank Paino. I'm editing a new anthology of fifty poets.

I have had some odd dreams during these days. Being quarantined has shifted my focus on a number of life issues and things of importance, but most importantly, it's allowed me to focus a magnifying glass on what is unimportant.

One night, I dreamt about my old boss from thirty years ago. We were in a large concourse terminal for airplanes or a rail train with people bustling all around, and as I neared the escalator to go around to the Starbucks, my old boss and an older woman stepped in front of me *en route*. He and I said hello to each other, but the woman said nothing. I looked her in the eyes, and I knew she was his escort. She had him firmly by the arm and was taking him down the escalator. I woke, startled, knowing he was descending into Hell and she was not a woman but something sinister. All morning long, I felt uneasy, that maybe my old boss was in trouble or had died, and in my dream, he had been descending into the dark depths. I searched to find any information on him, an obituary, anything. Nothing popped up for a few days, and then he posted some photos on Facebook.

I had another dream about a childhood friend. I was selling a baseball autographed by Roberto Clemente on eBay, and, it turned out, my old friend was the buyer. I called him on the phone and asked, "Do you remember me from when we were childhood friends?" I woke up without an answer.

I have never liked conformity or authority figures telling me what to do. I don't even like an usher telling me where my seat is located. *Get the hell out of my way—I can find my seat without your help.* Yes, I get along quite nicely with most everyone, unless you are an authority figure, which seems to be *the* issue in the dreams. Apparently, in my dreams, I'm the type of person to tell you and the cops to screw off, which has caused trouble for me over the years. And, yet, here we are, seven billion people in the world, and most of us are home alone with some government pinhead telling us what to do because they know better. I never figured out one particular dream, but I woke with the sense that I had succeeded in winning some traffic ticket situation with the cops.

Have you ever dreamt that you were at Woodstock in the rain on Max Yasgur's dairy farm? I did just the other day. But it wasn't during the music festival. Some folks were showing me around the barn and the animals, telling stories about what had happened back in 1969. Maybe that stemmed from my idea that I would like to metal-detect that entire area, even though I have never used a metal detector before. I woke that morning feeling as though I had been to the farm. Maybe my spirit transcended my body and I was at Max's farm. I've often wondered about things like that—can we leave our bodies and float to another place, then return before morning? The feelings of being at Woodstock and petting the goats and breathing in the smells of the farm, they were so real that I could not shake that sensation throughout the day. I felt connected to the place, but also to 1969.

I was never a flower child or a fan of the counterculture revolution, although I saw it all the time as a child. There were parts of it I liked: the music, the ecology movement, naked girls running through wheat fields, psychedelic movies, the British Mod-look, tie-dye T-shirts, long hair (but not mustaches), bead necklaces, VW Beetles (not the buses), bellbottoms, and other *cool* things. What I did not like were sandals, communes, looking like I needed a bath, and most importantly, drugs. I liked Jefferson Airplane but not the Grateful Dead.

Do Your Own Thing was a 1960s mantra. After a while, it becomes a part of you, so you no longer need to say it. You simply live it. I figured people were doing what made them happy. I feel we have lost that feeling—to allow others to do their own thing, especially if we disagree with them. Facebook and Twitter are now utilized for telling people what they cannot do. Of course, these social platforms did not begin that way, but people have hijacked their original intent. Why can't people simply disagree without the venom? You do your own thing, and I will do my own thing. Seems simple enough. I remember a picture of John Lennon and Yoko Ono holding a white sign with black letters: "Don't Hate What You Don't Understand." When I was a kid, I thought hippies were cool even when I did not want to be one. I loved Peter, Paul and Mary and other folk music, and Haight-Ashbury was on my bucket list to visit someday.

I remember standing in my front yard in Pennsylvania, having an argument with the girls across the street. We could not have been more than seven years old. We were just yelling and screaming at each other. The argument: Nixon versus Humphrey. What in the world did I or these three sisters know about politics beyond what we'd heard our parents say? And, yet, there they stood in the street while I dug my *political* heels into the grass. I was in the Humphrey camp, while they were the enemy. *How in the world could they vote for Nixon?* All I knew, in my naivety, was that Nixon was bad. It was, of course, more complicated than that. For a school project, I had written to the president asking for a picture, which months later arrived in the mail. It was Nixon and his family. Had Tricky Dick really autographed it? Probably not. It was probably some intern. But out of all this, in 1968—one of the craziest years in American history, with the assassination of Martin Luther King, Jr., and Bobby Kennedy, and the Chicago riots—it was the beginning of where I stood in relation to how I saw the world.

I am writing this now because the quarantine has provided time to flip though old yearbooks and reflect about my youth. The world I knew as a kid has become vapor. I loved the Earth Movement, but none of us were budding Greta Thunbergs, whose current popular message I kind of agree with but not entirely. I also think she is a petulant brat cast upon the world stage by some puppet masters. Am I being tough on this young woman? Not hardly. If you stick your butt up in the world, expect a salvo of arrows. I read last week where someone said she was impersonating an autistic child. That's harsh. At age seven, there we were, arguing over who was better and who was going to win the election—Humphrey or Nixon. In a matter of seconds, we shifted from political enemies back to friends laughing and talking and eating PB&J sandwiches my mom had made. And, by the way, MLK became one of my heroes, while the more I learned about the Kennedys, the more I despised that entire clan. Yet again, the duality of the world.

What does all this mean? My weird dreams? My reflections during a pandemic? Back in the day, before social media, news traveled more slowly, but it seemed like every day on the news, there was a new mantra emanating from college campuses. Here are the ones I remember from the 1960s counterculture:

Do Your Own Thing

Make Love Not War

Explore Your Inner Self

Drop Out

Along with the word "Groovy," I remember television and radio shows and my older cousins talking about these things. I was too young to put them into action, as I did not fully understand what they really meant, and if I had, I had no way to implement them. Did I live by them? No, not with any sense of purpose or comprehension. At seven years old, I was just starting to play baseball with serious intent. Did I think about them? Absolutely, because I wanted to be cool and be accepted, and I wanted to go around to people saying, "Peace." I realize now that as I grew, I worked within the confines of all of them to some degree, but the one I have come to admire and use as a personal mantra is *Do Your Own Thing*. What does that mean in the time of quarantine? In the time of social media? In the time of universal hatred for opposing views?

For me—perhaps not you—it means being different and having diverse values and opinions and thoughts about the world. Doing your own thing also means allowing others to do their own thing, yet accepting them and not castigating them into silence even if you disagree. One of my best friends, Dan Franklin, and I rarely agree on political issues, but we have the most engaging conversations without explosive venom. Ours is an intellectual exchange of ideas, and even when we disagree, we are still friends. Why? Because we are adults. We like each other's company. Are we expected to agree, lockstep 100%? Absolutely not. I don't agree with my wife 100% of the time, so why would people expect everyone on the internet and in life to be so harmonious? As the sign said, "Don't Hate What You Don't Understand." For instance, I hate tattoos. I don't like piercings, either, but I'm not going to tell anyone they cannot get a tattoo, or fifty. I met a guy a few weeks ago, and when he asked what I did and I told him I was writing a new book, he said, "You know the last book I read? Never." *Fine*, I thought, even though I disagree with his lack of personal fulfillment. *Do your own thing.*

What have I discovered during the quarantine? During this time of confinement, I was reminded of when I was in the sixth grade in Mrs. Robinson's class, and, for a science project, Linda Aaron and I decided to clean up Rawhide Creek. With large trash bags and neighborhood kids trailing behind us, she and I were avatars of the ecology movement pulling a red wagon. It took most of a Saturday to fill those bags. With me pulling that wagon seven blocks up the hill on Longmeade Drive and Linda pushing, we were exhausted after such a long day. On Monday morning, we pulled the wagon to school to show Mrs. Robinson our efforts. Linda and I were twelve—she was older by five weeks—but what had happened while cleaning the creek had been greater than the ecology effort itself. What did I know about girls? Not much, having grown up in a house of all boys, but while cleaning the creek, we'd had hours and hours to talk about anything. I don't remember the details of our conversation, but I remember just talking endlessly while engaged in a cleanup effort and trying to keep little kids from falling into the water. We ended up being babysitters to those small kids who had simply tagged along. Their parents may not have even known they were with us. It was a time when kids simply left the house to play and returned at dinner. They helped pick up trash, too, and got to hang out with the older kids. She and I were out doing our own thing, cleaning up the creek, talking and having a great time. It was on a personal level, not distanced by web-technology. I learned a lot about what her life was like, and I suppose she learned about mine. It was like *The Wonder Years* without the infatuation between Kevin and Winnie. There was a shared goal of cleaning up the environment. When life is lived on the personal level, the perspective and interaction changes.

What have I done during the pandemic besides the deep contemplation of *Doing My Own Thing* and allowing others the same privilege without casting judgment and scorn on social media? I've reflected. But most importantly, I've realized I have too much stuff. I own more stuff than I can ever enjoy. I won't even list what it is. It's STUFF I will never use again but, for some reason, feel the need to keep. Does it make me feel good to own so much crap? No. I've realized, while quarantined, that I am bogged down by owning too much stuff.

I used to be a minimalist. What happened to that guy? During the quarantine, I decided to purge my life of stuff, which resulted in Craigslist and eBay being my places of choice to unload my burdensome junk. Not all of it, of course, but a boatload. When listing it on eBay, I did not care if it sold for $5 or $500. I had a reel mower I would have taken $20 for, but it sold for $300 on Craigslist. The goal was to shed the encumbrance of owning all this stuff. Perhaps my reading and studying Thomas Merton's *Seeds of Contemplation* during this time of isolation from the world was manifesting itself in the form of my personal enlightenment. What I think is important is not this stuff. I have, over the years, asked my college students, with the exception of pets and family members: if your house was burning down, what single thing would you take with you? *Nothing else matters.*

As devastating as the pandemic has been, I sense a paradigm shift toward "less is more," moving to rural areas and out of the city, simplifying one's surroundings, living a less complicated life. I know I will.

Years ago, David Letterman showed up in one of my dreams to hand out Top 10 ideas to me. He did not show up during the quarantine, but here is my new list:

Top 10 Alone Together Quarantine Revelations

1. Each of us is not the center of the universe. Although we are the centers of our personal universes, we can respectfully allow others to step into our circles.
2. The world is made up of too much stuff we do not need.
3. Adults should be able to disagree without hating one another or trying to destroy the other person's life.
4. Being thrown into a world of deep introspection has cleansing properties everyone should experience.
5. Opinion is more persuasive when it is not a rant.
6. If we lost five billion of the seven billion people in the world, we would probably survive, and the animals and the ocean would be better off.
7. Prior to the pandemic, we were already living quarantined lives—iPods in our ears tuning out the rest of the world; distance learning; social media conversations and arguments; movies and TV 24 hours a day so we don't need to interact with people; video games; and more. Most of us should have had no issue with social distancing.
8. What is most important are memories—as poet David Bottoms called them, *Pocket Charms Against Oblivion*—and they are the only thing you take to Heaven.
9. We are individuals, alone in our thoughts, and ultimately, each of us in time will be alone in our deaths; however, while we are alive, Do Your Own Thing and allow the world to find you. If the world loves your thing, you will know, but if not, that is fine, too—just Do Your Own Thing. Be happy and don't worry what others think of you.
10. During the pandemic, I learned to spell quarantine.

JUDY FARRINGTON AUST

Sleep Magic

MERCY REACHED ACROSS THE BED, FOR A MOMENT—JUST a flash, really—surprised to find it not only empty but unruffled. She squeezed her eyes shut, resisting the certain truth that the dreamer never gets to decide when it's time to wake up. She wanted to go back, back to that shadowless state of being where Ted's hands had caressed her face, his body pressed hard against hers, evoking sensations that had been so tangible, so immediate, she shivered at the memory.

The dreams had begun soon after she'd dropped him off at Springer Mountain in North Georgia, where the 2,200-mile Appalachian Trail starts. That had been three months earlier, in February, before all hell had broken loose. It had been before coronavirus lockdowns, before she'd been told to work from home, before buying groceries had become a basic survival test, before she'd known she was crazy about Ted. Or maybe she was just plain crazy. Some days lately, well—some days, she thought she was probably certifiable.

Mercy and Ted had met at a dog park near his apartment just over a year before. It had happened when his yellow lab had intervened in a spat between an aggressive sheltie and Mercy's twenty-pound something-or-other. Hodor, the lab, was a natural mediator, wise and attentive. He and Ted were a lot alike: lean, strong, and instantly likeable. She'd readily agreed to look after the dog while Ted had hiked the trail. Mercy had glanced at Hodor, curled up next to her Mae, and he'd lifted his head to meet her eyes as though he'd read her thoughts. Those dark brown eyes, so like Ted's.

She flicked the gold charm dangling from a chain she'd hung on a lamp switch next to her bed. Her Phi Beta Kappa key. It had become the source of good-natured teasing after she'd once made a passing reference to her induction into the fraternity of over-achievers. Not that Ted was any academic slouch. He'd just earned his MBA with high honors.

He would be somewhere in Pennsylvania today, based on the map he'd marked and left for her. The last time he'd called, he'd been frustrated to find large sections of the trail closed because of the pandemic. He'd had to look for alternate routes, often walking along paved highways. Mercy had encouraged him to come back, to wait until things got back to normal, but he'd felt this was his one chance to do the thing he'd wanted to do since he'd been a kid. He was set to start a new job in the fall—and to start paying off sizable student loans. She dutifully shipped the supplies he'd wrapped and addressed, hoping he'd be able to retrieve them at the appointed sites.

What a god-awful mess it all was. Mercy looked around her bedroom—also a mess. She wasn't normally a slob, but she'd stopped caring about the clothes scattered on the floor and empty soda cans on every horizontal surface. She peeled back the covers and tugged on the yoga pants she'd already worn two days in a row, not bothering to change the T-shirt she'd slept in. Both dogs, familiar now with the routine, hopped to their feet, ears at attention, ready for a wake-up walk.

Mercy and the dogs were on the return route when she felt a buzz at her side. She reached for her cell phone and struggled to extract it from her tight waistband. *Damn*, she thought. She'd read about the "COVID 19," referring to the nineteen-pound weight-gain people were reporting. Maybe she should back off the bread-baking and the extra glass—okay, *glasses*—of wine for a while. By the time she got the phone, the screen read "Missed Call: Ted Dreyer."

"Dammit," she said out loud, gently bringing the dogs to a stop. She touched "Call Back" and held the phone to her ear as it began to ring. He answered right away.

"Hey," he said. Mercy heard something dry crunching under his feet, and his breath was punctuated with rhythmic puffs as he walked.

"Hey, you," she answered. "I'm out with the beasts. Where are you?"

"I don't exactly know, to be honest. Somewhere north of the Maryland/Pennsylvania line, but the trail is blocked off and I'm making my own way."

For Mercy, dangers far greater than viral exposure came to mind. Snakes, bears, running out of water, getting well and truly lost. He wasn't being bold—this was straight-up reckless. Mercy steered the dogs toward a flat, shaded rock and sat down.

"Ted, are you sure—?"

"I'm okay. I promise. I'm not far off the trail, and I'm keeping close track of my coordinates. I made it to a shelter last night and, God, it was a good night's sleep." He hesitated for a minute. "I had good dreams," he added.

"Oh yeah? I had a pretty swell dream myself," Mercy said. "You were in it, by the way." She said the last bit, then wished she hadn't.

"Hmmm." The sounds under his feet stopped. "I dreamed about you, too."

His voice was barely more than a whisper, and Mercy's breath caught in her throat. She paused, waiting for him to elaborate, but he didn't. The momentary silence pulsed with an edgy current.

"Ugh—'Nightmare on the Appalachian Trail,'" she joked finally, dismissing the notion that his dream might have been anything like hers.

He laughed. In the year since she'd known him, they had staked out a clear boundary of companionable—and unquestionably platonic—friendship. She hadn't thought of him as anything more, and she was positive he felt the same. The only thing that would come of elevating that relationship would be to ruin it altogether. Still, her heart had plunged.

A week later, Georgia's governor announced his "stay-at-home" order would be lifted and hair salons, gyms, and, of all things, tattoo parlors could reopen. When Mercy heard the news, she self-consciously reached to touch the ink on her back. She'd once dated a guy who had called it a "tramp stamp," and she'd never let anyone see it since. Whenever she thought of that guy—never fondly—she was bewildered that anyone would think a person nerdy enough to have a tattoo of a Harry Potter icon could be characterized as a tramp.

A week after Ted's call, a postcard arrived, postmarked in a town in Pennsylvania Mercy recognized only because it had been the destination for one of the supply packages she'd forwarded. The photo on the front overlooked a misty valley apparently untouched by civilization. She flipped the card over and read Ted's brief note written in his tiny, scratchy print.

> It's a thrill when scenes like this just appear out of nowhere. Thanks for the supplies. Wish I'd packed pasta and meatballs. Hell, I'd settle for a can of Spaghettios. Nice to hear your voice today. God, I need a shower.
>
> —Ted

That night, Mercy led the dogs to their bed, watched them circle before finally settling against each other, and wondered how they would consent to separation once Ted came back. She propped the postcard against the lamp on her bedside table and studied the image, watching the suspended key weave a slow shadow back and forth. She summoned the scent of the forest's pine-spice funk and wondered what he would be doing now.

The dream came in the early predawn hours. A much thinner Ted sat next to her on the edge of the bed and reached for the postcard. He looked at the photo, then turned to Mercy and pulled her close. His skin was cool and his lips were warm against hers, tender, as they always were in her dreams, as though he were savoring a delicate sweet, trying to make it last.

When she woke, the room was dark. The only sound was Mae's gentle snore. Mercy pulled back the cover and walked to the bathroom for a glass of water, which she brought back and drank, sitting cross-legged on the bed. An immense sadness rolled over her—an emptiness of longing unfulfilled. She set the glass on the table and lay awake in bed until horizontal bars of light appeared between the blinds on the windows.

For most of that day, Mercy nursed a simmering anger. Anger at the dream, at Ted, at their friendship that made the reality of the dreams impossible. It was irrational, she knew, but nothing about being isolated alone in her apartment was rational. She was still seething when Ted called.

"Hello, Ted," she answered, without intending the irritation in her voice.

"Hey there. You okay?"

"Yeah. And no. Just feeling sorry for myself. Sick of quarantine."

He exhaled audibly. "For a second I—well, yeah, I guess it's getting old."

"I'll survive. But how are you? *Where* are you?"

"Yesterday, I crossed the Delaware River and spent the night in Port Jervis, New York. Ten bucks says you never heard of that. I got a hotel room and took my first shower in almost a month. Best shower I ever had. And I got a bacon double cheeseburger and fries. I've taken in my belt a couple of notches—I definitely needed the calories."

"I don't doubt it. Glad you're making progress, though. I got your postcard, by the way."

"Yeah, I know," he said.

"How did you know?"

Ted hesitated, then said, "I guess I don't *know*—I definitely don't know. I don't—know why I said that, but I dreamed you got it. It was on your nightstand, next to a lamp." He laughed and added, "And your genius medal."

Mercy's hand went to her mouth. She remembered the dream, the shadow of the Phi Beta Kappa key. He'd picked the card up and then...

"When? When did you dream it?" she asked, purposely interrupting her own thoughts.

"Last night," he said. "Sorry—I didn't mean—it's not a big deal. It was the shower, I guess. Didn't I write something about how bad I needed one? Just forget about it."

"Well," she said, the words pouring out before she could stop them, "I dreamed about you last night, too. And in my dream, you were sitting on the bed, looking at the postcard on my table. And my genius medal is there, on the lamp."

"Seriously?" There was an urgency in his voice now. "That's exactly like my dream. And then—" He seemed to catch himself. "—yeah—that's all I really remember."

"Yeah," Mercy rushed to say, almost stepping on his words. "I don't either. What a strange coincidence, though. Just proves what they say about great minds."

"Right," he agreed, but his tone suggested his own mind was someplace else.

Mercy's hand shook as she poured a glass of wine a few minutes later. They had inhabited the same dream, or at least the first part. What if they'd shared the rest of it?

"Impossible," she said out loud, causing both dogs to look at her with upraised ears and heads tilted. "You heard me," she said to them. "Absolutely impossible." Then she downed half the glass in one gulp.

The next dream, a couple of weeks later, was nothing like the others. Mercy was deep into a fitful sleep, tossing in her bed and battling some indistinct stress, when Ted, filthy and almost unrecognizable, burst through the bedroom door and fell, bleeding, onto the floor. At the same time, her own body stiffened, and she realized with alarm that she was paralyzed. She tried to move, to go to him, but her arms and legs were frozen. He lifted his head, held out one hand, and begged her to help him, to come to him. She strained to reach out but could not move. As she watched, helpless, Ted gradually dissolved into the floor, leaving no trace that he had ever been there.

Mercy woke, shaken. She lay still—fully, painfully awake, trying to make sense of the nightmare. After a long time, she sat up and punched her pillow hard.

During the next two weeks, Mercy heard nothing from Ted, not even in a dream. At first, she worried they had jinxed everything somehow, with their talking-not-talking about the subconscious trysts. But when her calls and texts went unanswered, more unsettling possibilities crossed her mind.

Eventually, she reached out to Ted's roommate, Jerome. He was a medical intern with crazy hours and she was reluctant to bother him, but she didn't know whom else to call.

"Have you heard from Ted recently?" she asked, after brief how-are-yous.

"Not a word in weeks, and I didn't get his funds transfer for the rent this month. That's not like Ted. I've tried calling, but his phone doesn't even go to voicemail."

"He's not answering my calls either. I've been worried out of my mind."

"I'm sure he's okay. Just—how did he sound the last time you talked?"

"Like Ted. Normal—upbeat, even. But he's been going off-trail in places where it's closed. Oh God, what if he's lost? Or worse?"

"Seriously, I'm sure he's fine," Jerome said, sounding anything but sure. "Tell me where he was when you last talked and I'll make some calls."

After she hung up, Mercy went into overdrive, researching everything she could find about missing hiker protocol and rescue procedures. The next morning, she got on the phone herself, and by afternoon, National Park Service rescue teams were at work. Two days later, she got a call.

A pair of hikers had found Ted, barely conscious, at the bottom of a ravine. They had stopped to photograph a nest of owlets in a tree below and spotted him purely by chance. He'd been helicoptered to a hospital in Greenwich, Connecticut, but she was given no information about his condition. He was alive—that much she knew—and it would have to be enough for now. He was *alive*, and there was only one thing for her to do: find a way to get to him.

Mercy's efforts to book a flight were frustrated by severely reduced schedules. The virus had resurged with a vengeance, and flights were scarce. Given the option of two long layovers or getting into her car and driving the whole damned way, she figured she'd get there faster on her own.

She stopped by Ted's apartment to drop the dogs off with Jerome before leaving the city. Grabbing the leashes, Jerome handed her a grocery bag he'd filled with some of Ted's clothes.

"I figure he's going to want something clean to put on," he said. Mercy didn't know Jerome well, but Ted thought he was a great guy, and she was inclined to agree.

She made it to Greenwich in just under fourteen hours. It was surely some kind of record, aided by sparse traffic most of the way. A steady infusion of coffee and energy drinks left her exhausted and jittery at the same time. By the time she got to the hospital, it was mid-afternoon, and Ted had received discharge orders. Mercy gave the bag of clothes to someone at the information desk, and a half-hour later, Ted was wheelchaired to her car wearing fresh jeans and a clean T-shirt.

He looked pretty battered, leaning on a crutch, one arm in a sling. In the car, she reached across the console to hug him, and his frame felt sharp, but a strong free arm returned her embrace.

"God, I'm glad to see you," she said.

"Should have seen me before a shower and shave," he said with a wry smile.

They checked into a hotel to give Mercy a chance for catch-up sleep and agreed to share a room for the sake of economy. Somewhat awkwardly, Mercy asked the desk agent for two beds, and Ted indicated approval with a vigorous nod. If they were ever to broach the subject of the dreams, now was not the time.

Over room-service pizza, Ted told Mercy about how he'd wound up stranded at the bottom of a gulch. It had started with a confrontation by a pair of feral hogs on a remote section of the trail.

"One of them had tusks a foot long," he said. "No lie."

He described backing away slowly, only to be chased until he'd been able to hoist himself onto a low branch, where he'd literally spent the night in a tree. The next morning, his phone had been dead and he'd had no idea where he was or how to find his way out.

"It was almost a week before I found the trail again," he said. "I rationed my food and water, but by that time, they were gone."

Mercy noticed that he tapped two fingers fast on his knee as he talked.

Near desperation, Ted had heard flowing water below and, with no other obvious options, had started down a steep, rocky pitch to refill his canteens. But he'd lost his footing on the way down and tumbled to the bottom of the cliff, coming to rest near a creek.

"I thought I'd broken every bone in my body, to be honest. Sure felt like it. All I knew at the time was there was no chance of climbing my way out of there. I'm lucky to come back with a dislocated shoulder and an ankle sprain."

And two rows of stitches on your forehead, Mercy noted to herself.

He'd treated the creek water with tablets and scavenged hickory nuts; otherwise, they both knew, he likely would not have made it. He said that at one point, he'd hallucinated, and then he stopped in the telling and searched her eyes as though he were looking for recognition.

Later, Mercy helped Ted into bed, and then, still disturbed by the dire story, she crashed on her own bed and was out before the sun had completely set.

A sound in the hallway sometime after dawn disturbed her sleep, and she was confused, forgetting for a second that she was not at home. The dream—the happy one—had returned as real as ever, and she fought the inevitable awakening. Even as it grew faint, she imagined she could still feel Ted's illusory arm draped across her waist, his slow breath stirring her hair. Yet something was different. Besides the familiar warmth against her back, his legs tucked behind hers, there were other sensations: the whir of an air conditioner, an elevator dinging somewhere in the distance. She turned slowly, carefully, with a dawning awareness that this time it *was* real, that Ted, warm against her body, was real.

She opened her eyes and took in Ted's face, sweet in sleep, and inhaled deeply the scent of his skin, his hair. Her fingers brushed a bruised cheekbone, abnormally angular under bronzed skin, and his eyelashes fluttered before the lids opened slowly. He seemed surprised to be lying next to her, as though he, too, wondered about the reality of it. She touched her finger to his lips, feeling them as warm and soft as she had dreamed.

Without a word, he traced the length of her arm with his hand and brought it around to rest exactly where the tattoo was hidden under her nightgown. His eyes met hers, and his face broke into a smile.

"Lightning bolt?" he asked.

"What can I say?" She didn't need to ask how he knew.

Ted lifted his T-shirt just enough to reveal a pale image on his side: a winged Snitch—the object of the highly contested Quidditch matches in Harry Potter novels.

Mercy couldn't help herself. She laughed out loud, and once she started, she couldn't stop.

"We must be a pair of misfit soulmates," Ted said, joining her laughter.

Soulmates. She liked that—even the misfit part.

"So... what do a pair of misfits do now?" she asked.

"Seriously?" he asked, and he kissed her in a way he'd never done before.

Not in her wildest dreams.

ANNA SCHACHNER

Damn the Damndemic

Gina did not believe that front-yard signs announcing kindness or togetherness or thank-yous to essential workers did much good, even if children had painted the messages in bright, crooked letters surrounded by lots of hearts and smiley faces, so she bought ninety-six rolls of toilet paper on the internet instead. She clicked her mouse four or five times, and three days later, there it was—a cardboard box that she had to turn end over end to get up the steps and into her foyer. The box was the only guest she'd had in more than two months. She stared at it for longer than she should have, wishing she didn't know what was inside, which was dangerous. The wishing, not the not knowing.

"Damn, damn, damn damndemic," Gina said aloud. She traced her X-Acto knife down the middle of the shipping tape and popped open the box's lid. It was toilet paper all right. Individually wrapped, thankfully. She took out two rolls at a time, counting. She stacked most of them in the coat closet behind a black velvet swing jacket she had bought some years back, when she'd hoped to date yet again and finally marry—she'd figured her best chance was a widower with grown children she'd have to learn not to get too close to. Then she washed her hands long and hard and sat on her front steps, waiting for any delivery van at all, rolls flanking her sides, the flimsiest of arsenals.

A gray Prime van (no surprise there, since she suspected Amazon was more an army with sneaky surveillance than a company) was the first to appear around the side of the corner house where a family had recently moved in. The three little girls had hung flowers made of cut-up sheets of plastic from the crepe myrtle tree still months away from blooming. Gina stood up, a roll in each hand, waited for the van to stop in front of the Millers' across the street, and shouted at the driver, "Need any TP? A little gift to say *thank you.*"

The woman driver had one long, dark braid that bobbed up and down her back as she shuffled boxes at the rear of the van. "What you got there?" she called back, some interest—some suspicion, too—in her voice. And some lilting; a trace of an accent?

Gina opened her mouth to say, "toilet paper," but then: that blankness or maybe reluctance—not in her thoughts, which were just fine, thank you. In her words, or rather in her willingness to share words, to talk. If she answered back, it would be a real conversation with a real person. It had happened before, two days earlier, when she'd gone to her mailbox. A woman from the neighborhood out powerwalking had stopped, keeping her social distance, to ask if Gina knew a good handyman. Gina had started to say that she knew three who were all very good, one of them very handsome to boot, but she could hardly speak at all. She'd ended up saying only, "No, sorry," and then had watched the woman, arms pumping, until she'd gotten to the end of the street, maybe wanting her to turn around and come back to chat, maybe wanting that she had never stopped in the first place, not sure which would have ultimately made her feel more alone.

"Here," Gina shouted at the driver. She scurried to the curb, where she placed two rolls. Then she went to her bottom step and waited for the driver to leave the Millers' package before crossing the street to retrieve her gift.

"Thanks. Gonna put it to use, for sure," the young woman said, waving the toilet paper as she climbed into the van, and Gina heard the accent now. Hispanic. Gina looked away. As the van drove off, she wondered what the driver thought of her—some gray-haired lady with her knock-off Charmin—and she was almost grateful to think that she had been judged.

Before Gina turned to go back into the house, she glanced to see if the three girls were out playing. Yesterday they had run, cartwheeled, or danced between two lines of onlooking stuffed animals, and their squealy voices had been little bullets of joy. Her eyes never made it to the corner, though, because on the sidewalk four houses down, skinny legs walking, was a chicken. A chicken in a damndemic, strutting and clucking, out in the world.

Gina didn't know about other chickens, but this one had an agenda. No doubt escaped from a backyard coop, she was now preening—a mixture of freedom and snarkiness. She pecked. She thrust open her wings and wildly flapped them. She would not come. It took Gina two forevers to catch her, but when she did, she clutched the chicken against her stomach, both arms—a few specks of blood surfacing on each—locking her in, her tiny chicken head barely able to turn. Chicken contained, Gina started walking, slowly at first, unsure of everything beyond the confines of her house.

She passed seven houses on her side of the street, expecting the Franklins or the Garretts—no, probably those old hippies, the Shugarts—to intercept her and claim this rogue creature. Nobody did, though, and, sweat beginning to bead above her upper lip, Gina considered taking her home. She'd have to put her somewhere—maybe the back bedroom that never got used? In *her* house. Gina Gardner's. Six rooms of her, just her, these last few months, the walls closing in on—or was it taunting?—all the emptiness. The thought of it made her slow, made her remember and then push that memory away, the chicken's wings twitching beneath her arms.

Across the street, the front door of the corner house opened, and two of the girls bounded across the yard, yelling, "Mildred! Mildred!" and "You've found Mildred" and "Mildred escaped, but now she's found" and "Stinky ole Mildred," bare feet stopping at the curb.

Gina took a few steps toward them, ten yards or so away but still the closest she'd ever been. "Is this your chicken?"

The older one, who wore cut-off shorts and a messy ponytail high on the back of her head, said, "No. She's the neighbors'." She pointed behind her. "Miss Amy's and Miss Sheila's." She clapped her hands.

"Yay for Mildred being found," she added while her sister twirled in delight beside her. "Mildred will go *home*, right, Mildred?"

Gina looked at the girls and then pressed her eyelids tight against it. The memory—twenty-odd years old, now. Words, maybe not, but the memory had become urgent, ready. The little girl from Guatemala. Three years old with black eyes and a smile whose edges were hidden in pudgy cheeks. Deposits. Forms and signatures and a nice woman named Betty who'd come to visit, to look over her house and to nod approvingly at the back bedroom painted green, like trees. More deposits. Spanish phrases, new and just-right heavy in her mouth, r's she couldn't quite roll against her tongue. Tiny white socks with lace around the ankles in packages of three at Target. Telenovelas on *Univision* so she would know drama when she saw it. Her whole world crowded and full until one day, just weeks before her flight to meet the girl and bring her home, Gina couldn't do it. Just couldn't do it. What if the child resented her?

When Gina opened her eyes, the two girls were still, staring. Mildred, too, was looking up at her as though awaiting instruction, her red, fleshy wattles making Gina's own look minor. Gina crossed the street and stood six big feet from the girls. "Will you show me where Mildred lives?" she asked. "But perhaps tell your parents first."

"Okay," the younger one said, turning to run back inside.

The older one—she must have been about six—reached out her arms. "I'll hold her. She likes me, don't you, Mildred?" Gina hesitated, worried about the pecking, but the child was clearly not afraid. With all ten fingers clamped around Mildred's middle, she passed her to the girl, their hands touching, which both startled and amazed Gina. The girl pulled Mildred against her chest, giggling when the chicken squirmed.

With Mildred out front, the older girl led the way down the sidewalk and around the corner onto Dale Road, Gina in the middle and the younger sister behind her. Taking Mildred home was almost a parade, Gina decided, though she was the only one in it who knew fear, who had ninety-four rolls of toilet paper to prove it. Fear and regret, they were inseparable. She'd have to keep learning to live with the regret. But not the loneliness. Within the hour, the mail carrier would come. Once Mildred was returned, Gina could go home and push up the red arrow on the mailbox, in which she would place as many rolls as it would hold. Then she might do some of the usual talking to herself, only now it would count as practice.

Until then, as they walked, Gina wondered where the third sister was, but she didn't ask. Without even knowing her name, though, she missed her more than she could say.

SCOTT THOMAS OUTLAR

On Assignment

In the Age of COVID
we are breathless

enraptured by
the seizure of our
sneezing rights

and closure
quickly
of churches
holy

no chants, no songs
no sing-alongs
of hymns
arising Sunday

but you can take
to the streets
and scream
all you'd like

As you wish
my dear

the dread
of control-crazed
cults

comes canceling
without carols

Collective Hysteria

If I started to complain
I wouldn't know when to cease

I used to pick up trash on the side of the road
now even noble deeds warn of disease

What a good boy am I
what a monster are we

My Father
where art thou

In Heaven
heroes reward
of peace
well-earned

but here
on Earth
we sure could
use your judgment

Of Faith and Justice

And I have known you as a storm
suddenly summoned
not some measly plague

some masquerade
in the Wuhan Age

some fountain everlasting

Burn, baby, burn

Spin, sugar, spin

Hangman and hellfire

Hallelujah in the notes between

Blue pines are more forgiving, hum a song for every season. If you
can't scream, I will. Swear to God it all lines up at center. High tides
are brewed for healing, a grain of salt withheld. If you won't dream,
I will. Maybe recall a splintered fragment tearing through the void.

Nip It in the Bud

Everyone trying to save the world
might focus on their own lives first

Usually the case is solved
more closely drawn to home and heart

Blowing smoke signals from the woods
mostly my lungs bear the brunt

Not to be too blunt
but I know
they're not playing pretend
this turn

concerning utopia and revolution

-

July 12, 2020. The year of sacrificial rites. Roaring Twenties. With
bio weapons gaining function & unrestricted warfare rearing its
head. Dragon fangs. New Order Dynasties. Freedom wanes. In
Hong Kong the same as the streets of Seattle. Autonomous zones,
anonymous behind sanctioned masks. If life were a script it would
make more sense. But as it is, the next chapter remains ours to write.
The blessing of free will anchors mindfulness during a pandemic.
What an interesting time to be alive.

Sway

Out of contact
    (kisses & context)
  during corona
    spiked halo of fire

Speaking of futures
    (lockdowns & looting)
  absent governors
    four tires, no brakes

How have you been dreaming, darling?
What remedy of herbal tea?
Look at this that's left in ruin.
What rotten fruit of nihilism?

Here's the windup
    (egos & errors)
  selling hard labor
    like a Valhalla stroll

Promise the farm
    (media & newspeak)
  prospering faith
    holds steady, soft shift

SUSAN SANDS

Killing Grandma—
Erasing Our Mentors

DURING THIS TIME OF STRANGENESS, ISOLATION, AND LOSS, as we navigate the changes this novel coronavirus has wrought to our society, I can't help but grieve the loss of our old people—the parents, the grandparents of this world. Their sudden disappearance from this life is a tragedy we will only begin to understand in the years to come. They are our link to the past in all of this, and now they are dying by the thousands. Our history, our heritage, is being wiped out even as we are distracted by the news reports of illness, stock market numbers, and state re-openings.

My grandparents taught me so much and loved me so well. They're gone now, but I think of them, each one, as I prepare yet another family recipe, pull out my Paw Paw's antique magnifying glass to read something with small print, or appreciate a species of plant or flower.

My dad's parents were originally from Port Barre, Louisiana, a tiny speck along Bayou Teche, about six miles from Opelousas, Louisiana, where my dad grew up. We called them Mama Louis and Pappy. They were loud, passionate Cajun people. They fought, they laughed, and they were the best cooks of anybody in the family. For Pappy, if it lived on four legs or swam, he could prepare something spicy with gravy with it.

Pappy couldn't read or write and spoke only Cajun French until his teens. Neither of his parents spoke any English. Mama Louis understood every word spoken in Cajun French but had stubbornly refused to utter a word of it beyond her teens, because she'd been teased once over a pronunciation error as a young woman. They were quite a pair.

Mama Louis was a seamstress who sewed for the fine ladies in town from the late 1940s through the 1970s, when she and Pappy settled in Port Arthur, Texas. She made clothes for us growing up and even made my wedding dress in 1989 from a photo in a magazine and a basic dress pattern. She and my mom spent months beading and sewing, even through the death of my one beloved sibling—my brother, Charlie—three weeks before my wedding in May.

Mama Louis sewed Pappy's jumpsuits for as long as I can remember. One-piece, belted, zip-up jumpsuits, always with a matching "Pappy cap." She found fabrics that he called "loud." Brightly colored prints with large birds, letters, stripes, or flags on them. The louder the better. As loud as his personality. One of them, I remember, even glowed in the dark. I wish I could show you the photos.

Pappy played the guitar, the harmonica, and the French accordion. He sang Cajun French songs that none of us understood. Mostly when he drank whiskey. Which Mama Louis hated. She called it his slop. He loved garlic. Raw garlic. Mama Louis was also not a fan of that. So, he cooked outside on his grill and with his burner and large black iron pot a lot. Not to say she hated everything he did, just some things he relished enough to do away from her.

Pappy retired as a first and second cook on the *Texaco Maryland* oil tanker. He survived a fiery shipwreck in the New York Harbor in 1966 from which he jumped overboard with no life preserver, unable to swim, and was saved by a shipmate. He owed the man his life.

Pappy sailed the seven seas, quite literally. He had certificates documenting his voyages to the realm of the Arctic Circle, and he spent a good deal of time in the South Pacific. He was often gone three months at a time. He played cards, gambled, and sent home beautiful fabrics and paste jewelry from China for Mama

Louis that he purchased while away. He served in the Merchant Marines during World War II. The man had stories to share that were endless.

Since Pappy never learned to read or write, how could he hold a job as a chef on a massive oil tanker, serving three meals a day to a large crew? He developed amazing compensation skills and learned to estimate. And he always kept someone by his side to read for him, because he couldn't read a recipe. So, he never used one.

When he made gravy, he mixed flour and water in a jar, shook it, and slowly added it to the simmering meat drippings and sautéed vegetables until it was, in his words, "T'ick, t'ick, t'ick." Always three times, he said it. He didn't own a regular *th* sound. It was, "Go down d'er and get d'at." And of course, something was t'in or t'ick. I can hear him in my mind, both of them raising Cain about one thing or another.

They moved one mile down the red dirt road from us when I turned ten. Before that, my brother and I spent time with them in the summers in Texas, where Pappy shipped out. Being so close meant I absorbed so much of their love and humor and learned how to cook their way. No one could make me belly-laugh like Pappy. No one. His love of making us all laugh was his joy. I giggle now just writing about him. He called me "Slew-foot Suzie with the flour-sack drawers." Yes, that turned into just Slew instead of Sue.

Pappy fished in the quiet cove of the enormous lake only steps from their front door in his tiny aluminum boat with an outboard motor. He used trout lines to catch hundred-pound snapping turtles and equally huge catfish. If you were never treated to his catfish couvillion, then more is the pity. The turtle meatball sauce picante wasn't bad either.

Pappy hunted on foot or with his four-wheeler that he called "my wheel." Rabbits, squirrels, deer, turkeys, or pretty much whatever he could take down weren't safe. But be assured: whatever he killed went into the pot that night. And was probably served with rice and gravy and lots of cayenne pepper.

Sometimes he took a ride on his wheel when Mama Louis chased him out of the house. But he often brought back dinner from the woods out back or the lake.

Did I mention we lived slap in the middle of nowhere? Like, nowhere anybody's ever heard of in rural northwest Louisiana. Not even a town, just a rural route where the mailbox still sits on the highway and you walk to the end of your driveway to get it.

And Mama Louis and Pappy lived a mile farther into the woods, but on the water's edge, which was nice and peaceful. They couldn't hear the log trucks screaming by on the highway.

Every Christmas, Pappy bought me a box of chocolate-covered cherries as a gift. I never liked them, but I pretended they were my absolute favorite candies in the world because it was something he did special for only me, and he'd made it our tradition.

When I was very young, and before they moved close to us, Mama Louis gathered all of her grandchildren to visit for two weeks in the summers. There were ten of us. Sometimes we were all there for some of the days, but most of the time, there were six or seven at a time. Mama Louis and Pappy lived in a tiny two-bedroom, A-frame house with a swing on the front porch. But they had a yard in front and in back, with an empty lot on the left side facing the street with two huge tree stumps. Spanish moss hung from the trees all around, and the grass was that thick-bladed, soft St. Augustine variety only found in certain places around the semi-tropical South, where the mosquitos are legend.

Trucks came every evening just before dark and sprayed for mosquitos. But let me tell you, there were still mosquitos and mosquito bites, which we treated with Dr. Tichenor's antiseptic. The strange people across the street had a courtyard all around their house and kept a horse right in the middle of the neighborhood. A girl named Karen, who was my age, lived next door. But my cousins, mostly girls of all ages, and mostly older, fascinated me. Some were from New Orleans and had strong accents, which furthered my interest. Mama Louis assigned everyone a job to help with cooking and cleaning.

We stood on tubs turned upside down to reach the sink and wash dishes. We laughed and sang silly songs. We baked cookies and cakes. We played checkers and Chinese checkers, and my cousins taught me all the card games. So many games. I have no idea where everybody slept. The little sunroom with the rollaway bed, the sofa, a mattress on the floor... maybe the front porch.

Mama Louis taught us all to sew Barbie doll clothes, to make purses, and to crochet. I mean, she even let us use her precious sewing machine. When I was the youngest, she used to rock me at night and sing "A Bushel and a Peck." She had a certain smell that I will never forget. I remember she had a bookshelf headboard on one of the beds where she kept her *Reader's Digest Condensed Books*, and I have to say, one of the most memorable reading experiences was falling into *The Secret Garden* through one of those books.

I think it was the first time I ever had the absolute joy of reading immersion. I must have been around seven. The beauty and safety of being tucked next to my grandmother reading at night after an exhausting day of Coppertone suntan lotion, running through the grass barefoot, and a hot bath is something I wish upon children of this generation.

Mama Louis read every night before she went to sleep, just before saying her rosary.

There was a guitar, harmonicas, and even an accordion. I don't remember anything being off-limits to us. We picked blackberries along the railroad tracks behind the house, discovered honeysuckle and sampled the taste of the nectar, and designed moss trails on the grass and pretended they were our houses. I guess you had to be there.

During this time in my young life, my creativity was given full rein. I soaked up every amount of teaching and knowledge offered me. This learning from my grandparents continued throughout my lifetime. I called Mama Louis and Pappy for cooking advice after I grew up and moved away. I wrote down their recipes over time. I visited as often as possible when I went "home."

The richness of my personal experiences with my grandparents cannot be communicated. This love between us cannot accurately be shown with my words. They loved me and showed me in every way. We lived so close, which meant my brother and I were the ones who benefitted the most.

I've always been extremely close to my parents, so y'all know I'm not leaving them out. I'm focusing on grandparents. My mom is my best friend, as is my own twenty-one-year-old daughter. And she and her grandparents are close, as well; the ones she has left.

Now, LET ME tell you about my mom's people. For most of my life, my maternal grandparents lived next door. They weren't loud. My grandparents met when they were ten years old. My grandmother and my mom were the very best of friends. My grandmother was a short, lovely dumpling of a woman who attended Mass with my grandfather every Sunday; in fact, so did my mom, brother, and I. My dad didn't go to church, but he thought our going was just fine.

They cooked Sunday dinner, and often the parish priest came and ate with us, something I hated with a passion. I mean, who wants the priest, who heard your confession the hour or so before, to sit across from you at dinner? Don't let that little dark booth fool you. They know who you are and they remember what you did. Factoid: I'm not Catholic anymore, but I still love Catholic churches, especially the old ones when they are dark and quiet. The smell of incense and the stained glass still bring me peace. Plus, the history is fascinating.

In North Louisiana, we Catholics were scarce, as it was, and still is, an almost wholly Protestant area. All the fun stuff happens below the tiny town of Bunkie in the middle of Louisiana. The beauty was, my entire family was originally from the "fun" part of the state, the part that knew how to cook and didn't mind a little dancing and drinking.

We called my grandmother Maw Maw and my grandfather Paw Paw. Not so exciting as the others, right? Well, there's something to be said for having your grandparents next door throughout a childhood. I was uniquely loved and spoiled in the best ways—with love all around.

Paw Paw kept a two-acre garden, fig trees, and a massive compost pile. They made strawberry fig preserves every year. We had purple-hull peas, strawberries, green beans, corn—you name it. We never threw away banana peels and the like because they went to be composted by hand.

Paw Paw ordered vitamin supplements through catalogs he found in ads in his *Organic Gardening* magazine. He always had some kind of potion to treat our normal cuts, bug bites, and scrapes. He even concocted his own wine in the refrigerator with tubes, putty, and a cork. I remember thinking it looked like a science experiment. But it wasn't shocking or surprising, as Paw Paw seemed to always have something odd brewing. He attended school until the eighth grade before working in New Orleans in the graveyards with his step-dad, building gravestones and tombs.

I grew up living near and learning from my grandparents every day of my life. We ate organic-farm-to-table and had fresh fish from the lake in the freezer at all times. Even into my forties, I was in close contact after I moved to Atlanta, as they all lived to their mid-nineties, save one. I learned to cook, craft, plant, sew, crochet, and so much more from them.

Maw Maw became ill with Lupus for several years, so she taught Paw Paw how to cook and organize everything in the household before she died. He mourned her terribly but found happiness in his eighties with their old neighbor, Clementine. After Clementine passed, he married her sister, Una. Paw Paw retained his faculties until he underwent open-heart surgery at ninety-four years old. He died at ninety-six, but he spoke to me on the phone the night before he passed and asked me to please be careful on the road heading back to Atlanta, as I'd come to visit and had spent several days and nights with him at the hospital.

I've introduced my childhood in this essay to make a point. We lived out in the middle of nowhere. We had little in the way of money or outside entertainment. There weren't a lot of other people around on a daily basis. We were—as some might say—alone together.

The very people who made the experience of my childhood so rich and who were so insightful in my lifetime are those we are killing right now. Our mentors. Our teachers. Who are we without their wisdom?

MY MOM IS seventy-five. She's just recovered from a big back surgery and a subsequent fall the day after she returned home from the hospital. Thankfully, it was a mere month or so before the COVID-19 virus made its way to our country.

I can't imagine life without my mom. Even though she's seventy-five, she drives, she lives alone, and she bakes me cakes on my birthday and brings over things she's cooked. Timing was everything when it came to her recovery. She has high blood pressure and takes an impressive amount of cholesterol medication.

So, at risk for COVID-19? Yes, definitely.

But she won't stay home. She's out at Kroger during senior shopping hours and then, often, off to Walmart. I don't blame her for wanting to get out and live her life, but I don't think she gets how contagious this is. You're not keeping that good woman down, Corona! People from her generation have worked hard their entire lives and endured much hardship. They don't see how a stupid virus could get them down. I, on the other hand, rarely leave my house.

I think if she were forced to stay at home *all* the time, it would kill her spirit. She might actually become ill. Staying still in her one-bedroom apartment, staring at the television, would be a dying of sorts. Maybe that's why she refuses to stay home. "COVID-shmovid" is her motto.

My dad died with dementia. It was the most horrific thing I've seen. It's gradual and terrifying for all involved—like a train wreck in slow motion. Really slow motion. The disease sucked the life from him and putrefied his comprehension and cognitive abilities. His memory. It gave him bloody-murder dreams and waking horrors and delusions. It pulls life and energy from the caregivers and loved ones until the bitter end. My mom cared for him constantly for several years, until he became a fall risk toward the end.

Will I die from dementia, like my dad? Do I want to know now? I think not.

My dad built things with his hands. He repaired pretty much anything that broke when we were kids. He knew a *lot* about a *lot* of things. My kids know almost nothing in comparison when it comes to using their hands and getting dirty. They are city kids. They played sports and video games. They use computers and hand-held devices. They call repair people when things break. People like my dad.

My husband, their father, is a dentist. A useful trade, to be certain; one that is high on the income scale and low on the doing-other-things scale. Golf, yes; fixing things around the house, no. My two boys and my daughter grew up close to my parents, but not close enough, physically, to learn from their grandparents the same way I did from mine. My dad took them fishing when they were very young. When they visited, or when we did, the visits were short, so there weren't weeks at a time spent doing all the things they might have together. My parents worked during the week when my kids were young.

My husband's dad was military and a retired professional bowler, so they have some skills in the bowling department and their own bowling shoes and balls. My middle son has a coin collection from his Papa John, who was a big gift-giver. Their Nana is still very crafty and is an excellent cook. My daughter has a doll collection from her Nana.

Fortunately, my mom and my mother-in-law are now living here in Atlanta. All my kids are somewhat local, so we are fortunate to have the moms nearby.

HERE'S WHERE I get philosophical. What happens when an entire generation of our parents and grandparents gets wiped out in a fell swoop? All the knowledge? All the love? All the elbow grease?

I hear about people pulling out their sewing machines to make masks. Who taught them how to sew? To use a sewing machine? I can almost guarantee nobody learned the skill in home economics class in today's society. Nope. It was my grandparents, that's who. Or my mom and dad, who did things with their hands.

So many who are at risk are those who taught us how to sew. To cook. To craft. To knit and crochet.

I've not been burdened by the nightly quarantine cooking because I learned the skills from my older family members. But I worry for the coming generations. Who will they learn from? Are we still teaching our kids such survival skills needed during a pandemic?

Will they be able to whip out their sewing machines and make masks? Will they own sewing machines? Unlikely. They have the internet.

I have a sewing machine and have always owned one. I bought one for my daughter when she asked for one as a teen. I encourage creativity of any kind. She has hardly used it, but I want her to keep it in case she ever decides to learn to sew. Or finds herself in need of it during another pandemic or worse.

The elderly so often believe themselves irrelevant because we treat them thusly. As though they no longer have anything valuable to offer the world, or even those around them; their loved ones, to be honest. Yes, I get that many are failing mentally and physically, but I'd like to think that, with a little prodding, there's still some grandparent magic there. That knowledge to pass along to us.

And they're dying in droves, y'all. Even if there wasn't a pandemic, the finality of death is stunning. Every time. No matter how deep your faith for meeting again in another life, it hurts to lose a loved one in this life. And the effect on another's life is forever.

I don't know the answers to any of the questions, just so you know. I simply want to focus on the questions. The aloneness our beloved seniors often face is heartbreaking. Maybe they don't have children to visit, or maybe they do. The stories I've read and heard of elderly folks confined to their single rooms in facilities break my heart. No sunshine. No human touch. No exercise. The helpless lack of control they must feel on a monotonous loop, where nothing changes and nobody knows when it might.

The sum of a life lived should not end like so many are ending right now. Even before this God-awful virus. We are a world of self-servers. We want what we want and we want it now. No sacrificing and no waiting. My parents and grandparents were sacrificers. They were patient, kind, and willing to do whatever it took to care for those less resilient. For years, if necessary. How do we get back to that? Did we believe a pandemic would teach us a lesson or two? Clearly, it did not.

So what if grandma has to go? She's lived a good, long life.

She's taught us how to sew those masks and cook so we can survive lockdown.

But will we, as a society, miss her? Or keep her special recipes?

Will we pass along the teachings our elders taught us so that our children learn lessons? Or will this all stop with our children?

The Magic 8-Ball tells me the outlook's not so good.

MOST OF US love our people and want to do what we can to keep them safe and not so alone. Sometimes, they prevent that by their own practices. But the sadness of this pandemic and its effects on the elderly, who are fragile and cannot control their own destinies, have deeply touched me.

We are better together when we can be, but never better lonely. Don't let anyone be lonely.

So, call your grandma and grandpa if you still have them. You are very lucky.

◇◇◇

Written in loving memory of my four beautiful grandparents.

ELIZABETH MUSSER

Confined in Spring

May 30, 2020
Atlanta, Georgia

THE SIREN JERKS ME AWAKE, LOUD, BOISTEROUS, IRRITATING. I glance at my phone. 2:30. I pull myself out of bed, go to the window, and look down, far down, to where the swimming pool gleams bluish-black in the floodlights on the seventh story of my building.

A text beeps on the phone. *Fire! Ground floor of Building One! Stay in place.*

I stare at the text. *Stay in place?* When there's a fire twenty stories down from me and sirens screaming through the night? I think maybe I'm dreaming. *Shelter in place* has become the most used phrase in America—heck, in the whole wide world—for the past eight weeks. Shelter in place and COVID-19 are practically the only words I hear these days.

And something about toilet paper.

I stare at the phone screen as text after text flips past, one underneath the next.

Fire

Looting. Broke the windows in the jewelry shop.

I heard gunshots.

Me too.

My condominium complex is lighting up my phone screen with comments. I start to type something and hear a sound in the hallway.

I grab my robe and pull it over the T-shirt that I've been wearing day and night. No bra, either. I've figured out how to do the Zoom calls with my boss from the neck up.

I open my door, and the hall is filled with masked people. I'd think looters had arrived on the 20th floor if this were not the new normal. I duck back inside and find my mask—a lovely floral design stitched by my elderly neighbor—put it in place, and return to the dimly lit hallway, its neon light casting an eerie glow across the forest-green carpet.

My neighbor, Grace, stands the required distance from me, eyes wide. "The looting moved from Lenox Square to Peachtree Place. It's right here!"

"And there's a fire." This from Caleb.

"Shouldn't we evacuate?" I manage.

Just then, all our phones beep in unison, like one of those online choirs that have been entertaining us for the length of confinement. *Do not leave your apartment. Do not evacuate. The riots are on the street below. The fire is under control. Stay inside.*

Eyebrows rise while a half-dozen sets of eyes, every color, all register one thing above the masks that cover our noses and mouths. Fear.

Mine is an upscale building. They've always handled problems well—efficiently. But this isn't merely a problem. It's a crisis.

Our phones sound six different ringtones, and our scared eyes are riveted once more to the screens. *Building One has been evacuated to the underground parking lot. Residents of Building Two are to remain in the building, in their apartments. Police order.*

We turn from our phones and stare at each other. I feel like a crewmember of the starship *Enterprise*. We've just been told that a meteor is heading our way, nothing we can do to avoid it, but don't worry. Just shelter in place.

*

BACK INSIDE MY condo, I slip the mask off, wide-awake. I consider calling one of my friends in Atlanta, but they are tucked safe in their beds, asleep, or should be. The rioting began in the evening, and most of us sat glued to the TV or internet as it unfolded downtown. No one expected it to make its way all the way up to the part of Peachtree where I live. So we all signed off from our texts and tweets around midnight.

But not all of my friends are asleep.

I text him. It's almost nine a.m. in France, but I know what his days are like. I pray for an answer, but nothing,

A hard knot sits stubbornly in my stomach. I spend the next hour swiping through texts on my phone, texts from the only other people awake: my equally terrified neighbors.

What should we do?

Is it safe to go into the hall?

Has the fire been put out?

At least we're in this together.

Yeah, alone together. How weird is that?

I'm dozing again when my phone rings: a *bona fide* call. I answer, seeing the number displayed on the screen.

"Hey! Just got off the night shift. What the heck is all this chaos in Atlanta—it's made the front page in *Le Monde*. Then I saw your text. Are you all right?"

I want to cry with relief. I yawn and feel some of the heaviness, the oppression, fall away at the sound of his voice. "I'm sitting here scared stiff. Told to shelter in place while who-knows-what is happening below. This is one more layer of 2020 surreal," I whisper.

He knows his role well. *Talk Elise off a ledge.*

So he starts talking, that ruggedly reassuring tone that nonetheless makes my insides flutter. He repeats information he's shared with me a dozen times on calls, but it works to distract me. "The French, no matter how typically rebellious they are, obeyed

Macron *à la lettre*. No leaving home except for hospital, pharmacy, grocery story, or exercise within a kilometer of the house." He takes a breath. "Now that confinement has lifted *un peu*, well, they're not quite as obedient." He gives a forced chuckle, which usually means he is only half-coherent, the fatigue heavier than the muggy Georgia summer air.

"Here, we have no idea who to listen to or what is real. I half-expect to come down with COVID." I am also repeating the same information he's heard a dozen times. "And now this."

This is the rioting that disrupts Atlanta in the wake of the murder of George Floyd. Always seen as the bastion of peaceful protests, Atlanta is losing her reputation in one crazed night.

"I'm terrified. No one is told anything except to stay in place. The news keeps running the story of the riots downtown, around Centennial Park. But it's radio silence for what's happening here."

"Are you okay?" he asks again. He knows that I'm not, but he needs me to admit it.

"No. But I haven't had another panic attack."

"Listen. I want you to write it all down. Everything since the beginning of confinement, exactly how it happened. Write until you drift off. I'll call you back at 7 a.m. your time. Write and sleep."

I can tell that he's scribbling out the prescription in his mind. If only it were that easy.

"But…"

"Write what you know, Elise. Not just the craziness. Remember all the good things you've told me about? Write those. Use your words. Take a deep breath and write about spring in Atlanta, write about the goodness you're seeing, the hope. Write hope to people who are desperate to hear it."

HOPE. WRITE HOPE? Really, Alan? That is about the last four-letter word that comes to mind right now.

But I'm not going to drift off into sleep, and I truly don't want to have one of my signature panic attacks.

So I open my laptop, watch as the screen comes to life, wallpapered with a photo of Alan and me, arms entangled as he takes a selfie of us standing beside the foreboding Fourvière Cathedral on a hill overlooking the city of Lyon, with its two rivers bisecting it.

For a moment, I'm back there with him and he's giving me a geography lesson. "There are three rivers that run through Lyon. Can you name them?"

I furrow my brow. "Three? Are you sure? There's the Rhône and the Saône, but…"

Then he's giving that rough chuckle. "Yes, the Rhône, the Saône, and the Beaujolais!"

"Haha!" Even I get the joke about the famous wine region that surrounds the northern limits of Lyon.

Alan is in his last year of residency in infectious disease through the Master of Public Health Program at Emory. The dream-come-true job landed in his inbox last March, when the world seemed sane. A year in Lyon, France, working with one of France's top *Professeurs*. "In many ways, France is kilometers ahead of the US in my specialty," he told me.

"Go. Of course, go. Accept it. That's awesome." But in my heart, I wanted to shout, "Stay here. Let's get married, and then I'll come with you."

Two years and three months of dating, and no ring. And we didn't do well with long-distance. At all. But I knew he'd regret this if he didn't accept. There was absolutely no reason not to. Except…

He moved to France in August of 2019, living with an elderly couple in the upscale 9th arrondissement of Lyon. The wife, Brigitte, fixed him four-course meals whenever he had a day off. *Escalope de veau et petits pois, coq au vin d'Alsace, spaghetti aux fruits de mer…*

"They can't wait for you to be here, Elise. You'll adore Brigitte and Jean, Honey." I liked it when he called me Honey. Or more recently, *Mon petit chou*, a French term of endearment. Something about a cabbage—or maybe a cream puff?

He wrote me long emails and we talked on Zoom for brief spurts, but his hours at the hospital were long, and when I got off work, it was well past midnight in Lyon.

I flew over and spent Christmas with him. I tried not to dream, but wouldn't France be a great place to propose? I'd take any nook or cranny in France. It didn't have to be Paris. I'd be thrilled if he passed me a ring while we stood in line at our favorite *boulangerie*, our mouths salivating for the hot *baguette* and the *pains au chocolat*.

But Christmas was… different.

Yes, the amazing Réveillon with Brigitte and Jean and a dozen other guests where the ten-course meal went on until three a.m. Yes, strolls together, bundled up and walking along the Rhône and the Saône. Yes, wine tasting in the Beaujolais beside the vineyards, perched on hillsides, naked branches just waiting to sprout in spring.

But his mind seemed distant. He pronounced the right words, but something seemed off. Something *was* off, and I left France with that gnawing in my gut.

When I finally managed to have *that* talk in February, he assured me all was well and bought me a ticket to join him for two weeks in April. Paris. Together.

Hope lurched up, and I pictured a proposal at the top of the Eiffel Tower or snuggled in a cozy café on the Left Bank. But COVID hit, and suddenly, instead of looking through a microscope, he was plunged into the horror of overcrowded hospitals and dying patients. He worked 24/7 at the hospital in Lyon, his job *essentiel*.

I sheltered in place 24/7 in my studio, sitting at my white Ikea desk, writing clever COVID copy for an online boutique that was going gangbusters now that everyone was shopping from home.

But Alan wanted me to write an actual story of how I was coping. He'd suggested this several times before, when I'd complained of how copywriting was drying up my creativity. His reminder served a twofold purpose now: to force me to get creative, and to keep my mind occupied so that I didn't have a full-blown panic attack. But I honestly had no idea how to describe the frantic feelings—the absurdity—of the past eight weeks.

It began with a downpour on March 16. I got caught in the thunderstorm in Piedmont Park, and, being soaked to the bone, I headed to my parents' house on Beverly, where I showered and changed into a pair of capris and a T-shirt I found stashed in my closet from childhood.

By the time I'd finished dinner with Mom and Dad, the news was calling for confinement. Governor Kemp had declared an unprecedented public health emergency two days earlier and ordered all schools closed as of the 18th. But then, the news kept getting more confusing.

Masks or no masks? Shelter in place for the medically fragile. Then for everyone. Mandatory? What about essential services? What about food?

During those early days of confinement, while I told Alan of a state of mass confusion, he explained the way the French stayed home and how at eight o'clock each night, many French threw open their windows, and, for two minutes, applauded all the health workers. "We started seeing the hashtags #OnApplaudit and #TousALaFenêtre. Brigitte and Jean are very faithful to applaud. She even bangs her wooden spoon on her *cocotte minute*."

"I think some people are doing that clapping thing here, too," I offered. But not in my building.

"On March 17th, we got texts on our phones telling us that we had to have an *attestation* to leave the house. There's a stiff fine for any infringement."

"A legal document?"

"Yep. Printed out, dated, signed, with the exact time you leave your residence. And you can only venture within a kilometer of home."

"That's a bit draconian, isn't it?"

"This is bad, Elise. You've seen the stats in Italy and Spain. We're right behind them."

"And these rules, are they enforced?"

Another chuckle. "On that first day, after receiving the text, I was at home—my rare day off. So I took the *attestation* and went for a jog—allowed—and was immediately stopped by the *gendarmes*. They're being very strict. It's like a cemetery around here. Or like those old-timey films that talk about the rapture. Everyone is gone."

On our Zoom call on April 3, Alan once again sounded not just tired, but off.

"My first time to have a patient die. I had to tell the wife." Unfortunately, by the middle of May, he had seen dozens of patients die.

Oh, Alan.

BUT NOW HE said, "Write about hope."

So I do. I remember the beauty of spring in Atlanta and how the internet is lighting up with photos of pink-tinted buds on cherry trees and sun-yellow forsythia and blood-red tulips. I think of the dogwoods in the backyard of my parents' home and their nail-pierced blossoms that speak of redemption every spring and the snow-white calla lilies growing beside their house, their faces turned upward like fragile trumpets calling for peace. I picture the lavender with its purple tendrils that spike toward a carpet-blue sky while bees busily buzz around each stem. As I smell the fragrance in my mind, I turn and write these words:

> **Confined in Spring**
> *How can I complain when I'm confined in Spring?*
> *When snow-white calla lilies curl towards the sun*
> *And lilacs bloom and tulips tilt their crimson heads*
> *And butterflies, like wind, like Spirit, flit to who-knows-where?*
> *When everything outside proclaims this simple truth:*
> *Life wins!*
> *So may I not complain but pray,*
> *Oh, yes, for all the dark and death that hovers 'round*
> *And pierces hearts and souls with fear and dread.*
> *Oh, may I pray with bended knee*
> *And bowed head*

That in the midst of this wild frantic thing
The fragrance of peace will come
And fill the fear with hope,
With courage and compassion.
May that sweet aroma of life
Whisper in such a fierce, victorious way
That many will turn an ear to hear
And listen, really listen,
To the whisper of the wind,
To Spirit's tug upon a heart,
And wonder if perhaps
That age-old Easter story
Might be true,
And, bending to inhale
The hope of cherry blossoms,
Believe.

I finish the poem as dawn shares its blush from outside my window, and I think how one terrifying night has been redeemed by words, first the words of a voice of reason from across the ocean and then by the words I write to assuage my scared spirit and remind me of truth.

Alan said, "Use your words."

I am not called to find a vaccine for COVID-19 or to end racism or even to stop the frenzied violence that is taking place on the ground floor of my apartment building. But I have a voice, and I can use my fingers to write a poem about hope and fling it out into cyberspace.

I end my post with prose: "We all have a voice. We can each be that voice in the middle of the night, across the hall, across the street, across the country, or across the ocean, reminding another of hope. We can each use whatever gift the skies have landed in our laps to share redemption and hope to this very needy world."

I finish my reflections and copy them onto my blog, surrounding the poem with photos Mom has sent me of her spring-filled yard.

I stifle a yawn as I post the story. Just then, my phone begins to ring. Alan's number. I take a deep breath, close my eyes, and answer with a smile.

"Hello?"

WILLIAM RAWLINGS

Fourteen Days

APRIL 1ST MARKED THE BEGINNING OF MY THIRD WEEK at home. By then, the days had started to seem routine: Get up early, feed the dog, go for a quick jog, then settle in by nine o'clock in front of the computer and phone, working on projects and fielding a variety of calls, the majority of which I referred to other departments. Around five, I would shut everything down and, weather permitting, sit on the back deck, drinking a beer or two before popping a frozen dinner into the microwave and watching Netflix until I dropped off to sleep. The pattern would repeat itself the next day, and the day after that. I'd wanted to visit my parents over the weekend, but they'd called to say that the rural North Carolina town where they'd retired had set up police roadblocks and was turning away "outsiders" seeking refuge from the virus.

Anna and I had been separated for almost three months. I was lonely, and the forced isolation was not making things any better. She moved out in early January—thinking about it now, I don't remember the exact date. She told me that she would be staying with her mother, that she would call me if she needed anything, and that I was not to try to contact her. I called anyway, of course, but was always greeted with a cheery, "Hi, this is Anna. Leave a message and I'll call you back." She never did.

It was the fifth year of our marriage. We met at a party in Savannah during the last semester of her senior year at SCAD. She was finishing up a degree in graphic design. I'd graduated from

Georgia Tech the year before and was down visiting a friend for a beach weekend at Tybee. We were both seeing other people at the time, but for some reason, we kept in touch. Three years later, we were married in a small ceremony on the beach at Tybee, near where we'd first met. By that time, Anna had landed a great job with a small firm in Atlanta. I was still working for AT&T, doing engineering and system layout for our larger corporate customers—mostly a desk job. We spent the first three years of our marriage in a small one-bedroom apartment, saving our cash to buy a house.

Over these past months, I have had a lot of time to think about things. I wonder now how couples make it long-term. Life is so random. We had things all planned out. We'd buy a house and have two kids. Anna would quit her job and stay home to take care of them. "You know, all I really want out of life is to be a good wife and mother," she admitted to me one night after a couple of glasses of wine. I do pretty well as an electrical engineer, so while it would have been nice to have two incomes, we could easily make it on mine. About two years ago, we took the plunge and bought a 1940s house in Atlanta's Morningside district, just north of Virginia-Highland and a short commute to both of our jobs. I work at the main AT&T building on the corner of West Peachtree and Ponce de Leon. Anna works for a graphic design firm near Emory that has found a niche in quickly putting together short-term ad campaigns.

Fixing up the house became the focus of our spare time. It sits on a wooded lot, with a generous fenced backyard sloping gently downhill. A great place for kids to play, Anna said. There are three bedrooms, each with a private bath, a one-car garage, and a finished lower level opening onto a small patio and the grassy yard beyond. We decided that we'd keep the larger bedroom for us and reserve the other two for the kids, if and when they arrived. In the interim, Anna, who had taken charge of things inside the four walls of our home, said I could use one of the two for a home office.

Within six months, Anna was pregnant. She was ecstatic, a ball of energy busily working on her new project of furnishing what had now become known as "the baby's room." She chose muted pastels in neutral colors, commenting that she'd "save the pink or blue for accent colors when we find out if it's a boy or a girl." We spent what seemed like an eternity shopping for a crib and a windup swing, as well as a single bed "so I can sleep in the room in case my baby needs me," Anna said. The results of the first ultrasound were encouraging. Dr. Brooker, Anna's obstetrician, assured her the pregnancy was progressing normally. The only disappointment seemed to be that she couldn't determine the gender of the baby. "Next time, for sure," the doctor promised.

Next time didn't happen. At what would have been the start of the fourth month of her pregnancy, Anna had a miscarriage. She stayed in the hospital overnight and was told to stay home for a week. Such things are not rare, Dr. Brooker assured her; perhaps a quarter or more of all pregnancies end in miscarriage. Most happen during the first trimester, "but you should be ready to try again in a month or so, if you want to," she added.

"We do," Anna said, her tone neutral as tears streamed down her cheeks.

This time, we waited nearly eight months before we decided to try again for a baby. Anna was fragile, no doubt, her days marked by a seeming lack of interest in the things that before had given her joy, and her nights by fitful sleep. Her internist tried her on a course of antidepressants. They helped. She showed improvement in just a few weeks and within a couple of months was back to her previous self. After two more months of therapy, he gradually tapered and stopped the medicine. Things seemed fine. Taking up where we'd left off, we tried again.

This time, it took less than three months before she emerged from the bathroom, proudly holding the dipstick with the two distinct lines confirming her pregnancy. Perhaps a little apprehensive, but eager to turn the page on the past, Anna once again focused on getting our home ready for the new addition. But as before, the unseen hand of fate struck another blow. Just after Thanksgiving, midway through the fourth month, she lost the baby.

After another overnight stay in the hospital and the same advice to "take it easy" for a week before returning to work, Anna and I were

once again at home, alone. Her mother, who has several health problems, offered to come by and help out for a few days. Anna refused.
Once again, she sank into a deep funk. I pleaded with her to see
her doctor, perhaps get back on some medicine. She refused that as
well. "This is so embarrassing... Just last week, when we were at my
mother's for Thanksgiving... everybody was there, congratulating
me on the baby. And now, now... I've failed again. And I don't even
know if it's me. It could be you. It could be that your..." She saw my
look and became suddenly silent.

"We'll work on this together," I said. "We'll get through it, I promise. I love you and we're going to make things all right."

With a look of despair on her face, she said, "Do you really believe that?"

It was now the Christmas season, but Anna refused to have any
decorations. For the first time in our marriage, she wouldn't let me
put up a tree. She discouraged my parents from visiting, making
excuses about not feeling well enough to entertain. It was clear that
she was depressed, but she was adamant in her refusals to consider
either medicine or counseling, or both. I tried to be supportive as
best I knew how, but she reacted to my efforts with a subtle hint
of hostility, as though the problem was in part or in whole mine.
"Think about it," she said, "the pregnancy—both pregnancies—were
half yours. Why should I take the blame for their loss when it could
be your fault?" I told her that no one was thinking about assigning
any blame. She scoffed at the idea. "I know what *I* want—what I
wanted—more than anything else in this marriage, in my life even.
The problem can't be all mine."

A few days after New Year's, Anna left. I came home from work
to find her gone, with a note on the kitchen counter that said simply,
"If I can't have babies, I'm going to find something to do with my life."
I called her cell phone but got only voicemail, followed by a text
asking me not to try to contact her. I called her mother's number out
of concern for her whereabouts. Her mother, who is always proper
and polite, told me that Anna was there and would be staying for
a while "until she sorts things out." "I'm so sorry, Tom; I love my

daughter, but I can't control her. I hope you two can get over whatever problems you're having. But please, for Anna's sake, don't try to call her. Give her some space for a few days..."

That was three months ago. I did check on her as best I could. I'm friends with a couple of her coworkers. They said she'd obviously been upset but was doing well at work and didn't appear to need anything. They advised me not to pressure her.

It was shortly after noon on April 1st. I was on the phone with an electrical contractor, going over the specs on a new network installation in Gainesville, when I heard the front door creak open and shut, followed shortly by a "thud" of something heavy being dropped on the entryway floor. I told the contractor I'd call him back and rushed out of my spare-bedroom office to find Anna standing by the door, a heavy piece of softsided luggage at her feet. "I'm back," she said. "I don't have anyplace else to go. But don't worry, I'll only be here for fourteen days."

For a brief moment, I was speechless, then, "Well... uh, I'm so glad you're here. I've missed you." A pause. "Do you, uh, need any help in bringing your things in? I'm..."

"I told you. I'll only be here for fourteen days—two weeks. Do you mind?"

Again, I didn't know what to say. "Uh... no, of course not. Why...?"

She cut me off. "The house is half mine, right?" I nodded. "Then I can stay here. I promise I won't bother you. I'll sleep on the single bed in the..." She paused. "...the other spare bedroom."

"But what made you come back today? Why didn't you call? I haven't spoken with you since January."

"The virus," she replied, hefting her bag up and heading toward what was supposed to be the baby's room. "Chad, one of the video guys at the office, has been sick for a few days. I've been working with him on a project. He saw his doctor, and they think he has COVID-19. They drew some blood for testing. I called Dr. Jackson, my internist. He recommended that I self-quarantine for fourteen days. And he's my mother's doctor, too. She's seventy-one and has diabetes and heart problems. He said that she's at high risk if she catches the virus—that there's a real chance of her dying." She dropped her bag and turned to face me. "Tom, I can't stay at my mother's, and I can't stay with one of my friends. I don't have enough money to stay in a hotel. So I came here. I have no other choice."

"But what about…?" I started.

"Work?" she said, answering my question before I asked it. "I was told I had to self-quarantine. I can do most of what I do online. You've got high-speed broadband here, so most of the time, I'll be out of your way, working on my laptop." She picked up the bag and turned toward the spare bedroom. "Fourteen days, that's all. Then I'm gone. I promise I'll try not to bother you while I'm here." She walked into the bedroom and shut the door.

It was a strange and uncomfortable situation, at least from my perspective. I had no idea what to do, how to interact with Anna. So, following her lead, I resolved to be polite but somewhat indifferent. Thus it was: the woman that I love, the woman that I married, the woman that should have been the mother of my children, living in the same house, both of us cooped up there for twenty-four hours a day and yet each of us trying to act as though the other were a casual acquaintance, simply another passerby on the road of life. It all seemed so painfully wrong.

For the first several days, we assumed the roles of polite strangers, perhaps two refugees from life whiling away the hours in a small isolated hotel in a third-world country. Through the wall of my office-bedroom next to hers, I could hear Anna on the phone, speaking with clients and running ideas past her boss, broken with long periods of relative silence when I presumed she was working on the computer. Sometimes she would talk softly to herself when absorbed in some online task, something she'd often done when we were together. So I was alarmed when I heard her say in a loud voice, almost a scream, "Do you really expect me to work on that?" Concerned, I knocked on her door.

"Are you okay?" I asked.

The door flew open. "They just assigned me a new campaign built around this slogan," she said, agitated. I gave a puzzled look and waited for her to continue. "I mean, I can't believe it. Why me?"

"I don't understand," I said.

"The slogan, it's the exact same thing you said to me that morning as you were leaving for work on the day I moved out." I said I didn't remember. She continued, "It's like a bad flashback. I just can't believe it…" Her voice trailed off.

"The slogan?" I asked.

"Your exact words."

She thrust a printout at me on which was written in boldface type, "We're All in This Together!"

"Those words have bounced around in my head ever since I left," Anna said. "And now, I'm supposed to figure out a way to show care-free people in quarantine, forced to… what? I don't know. Maybe I should just settle for puppies and balloons, and a backyard blue-sky sunset with happy music as a soothing female voiceover says, 'We're All in This Together!'" With that, she stormed back into the bedroom, slamming the door behind her.

At five-thirty, I shut down my computer and wandered back toward what we'd called the family room. The door to Anna's office remained shut. To my surprise, I found her sitting on the sofa, a half-empty glass of wine on the table near her elbow. She looked up at me with a soft smile. "I'm sorry," she said. "I owe you an apology for that outburst." She glanced out through the sliding doors to the deck. "It's nice outside. I opened a bottle of wine, if you'd like some." I followed her to find that she'd arranged two chairs overlooking the backyard. An open bottle of wine and an empty glass sat on the table between them.

It was a perfect afternoon. The temperature was in the mid-seventies and the sky was clear except for a few fluffy white clouds in the distance. At the far end of the yard, the late afternoon sun cast a soft glow on a bed of pink azaleas, now in full bloom. I poured myself a glass of wine and sat down in one chair. She sat in the other. After a moment of silence, Anna said, "Tom, I think there are some things we need to talk about." Her voice carried a tone of formality. I mentally tried to brace myself for what was sure to follow.

Anna looked at the sky, then the azaleas, then her glass of wine. She seemed to be thinking, assembling words in her mind before unleashing them on me. She began, "Uh… I just want to apologize again for the way I acted today." She hesitated, then continued, looking at me with a sad face, "I shouldn't have reacted that way, and I shouldn't have snapped at you like I did. I'm sorry." I waited for her to continue, but after a moment, she said, "It's really a nice day, isn't it?"

"It's a beautiful day," I replied. "Was there anything else you wanted to talk about?"

Anna took a deep breath and said, "No, not right now." The inevitable had been delayed, I thought. We both finished our glasses of wine, leaving the bottle half-full, each afraid that any more might loose a torrent of emotions. I asked about her work. She replied in terse sentences. She asked about mine; I said that I was keeping my head above water, though barely, hoping she caught the implication that it wasn't the work, it was my imploding marriage that was the problem. Rising from the chair, she said that she was going to fix herself a sandwich for supper and that she would put the half-empty bottle of wine in the fridge, if I wanted more.

For the next few days, Anna seemed pensive but less tense. On another fine evening, she suggested that we finish the bottle of wine. She'd ventured out to the grocery store that day and offered to share her pizza with me. "I know you're getting tired of your frozen dinners." We ate at the kitchen table in relative silence, but I did see her smile once at something I told her I'd heard about someone we both knew. There was a definite thawing in her attitude toward me.

During the first weekend after she moved back, we worked in our separate bedroom-offices. I had just been given a new project, and Anna said she was tied up with a rush job for a client. On Saturday morning, the 11th, the first day of her second—and last—weekend with me, I was surprised to hear her stirring about in the kitchen shortly before seven a.m. "You're up early," I said.

"I thought I'd take a ride in the country today," she replied, carefully placing two pimento-cheese sandwiches and a soft drink in a small cooler. "I need to get outside before I go any crazier."

"Oh," I said. "Do you need any company?"

She paused, looked up at me, and, after a moment, said, "No, I think not. I'm just going to drive up to the mountains for the day—maybe look at the early spring wildflowers. I don't think anyone's going to say anything about breaking quarantine. I'll be back before dark." She returned that evening about eight-thirty. I was watching TV in our old bedroom. I heard her come in, but she went to her room and shut the door without speaking. For the next three days, Anna was cordial but quiet. If she planned to follow her original plan, she intended to move back to her mother's on Wednesday, the 15th. On Tuesday evening, the 14th, she ate a few bites of supper, then retreated to her room. Nothing was said of her departure the next day.

I was in bed reading at about ten when I heard a quiet knock. Anna opened the door and walked in without waiting for my reply, sitting down on the edge of my bed. "Hey," she said. I replied the same. "I was planning on leaving tomorrow… I thought I should talk with you…" She seemed to expect me to reply, but I said nothing. "Tom, I haven't told you the whole truth. That first night, when I offered you a glass of wine on the deck, I wanted to tell you then, but I didn't have the nerve. I…"

"It's okay. I understand. I thought we had a good marriage, but…" I began, and she gently placed her finger over my lips to silence me.

"Let me speak, please. Late that afternoon, I'd gotten a call from Chad. His coronavirus test was negative. He said I didn't have to stay quarantined. I wanted to tell you that… but I realized if I did, I'd have to leave. Being here in our home, being around you, it's made me think so much about all that's happened, and about what a fool I've been, and about how much I love you. So I lied. I lied to you and to my mother. I told my boss that I was not feeling well, so I'd continue working from home for a while longer—he was fine with that.

"I blamed you for what happened with the pregnancies. I had crazy thoughts, like maybe you really didn't want to have children, or that you would eventually reject me because it looks like I may not be able to. So, I had this idea that we should get a divorce to set us both free, so perhaps we could start over… But the one thing that keeps coming back to me is what you said: 'We're all in this together.' You told me over and over that you loved me. That you wanted me no matter what. That you were here for me and that we'd work things out." She paused, looking down at the ring that had reappeared on her left hand. "Tom, I love you. Will you forgive me and take me back?"

Without waiting for my reply, she reached over and turned off the bedside light. In the darkness, next to her warmth, my tears flowed freely.

ROGER JOHNS

Honor Among Thieves

JOE HANNAH WAS NO LINGUIST, BUT THAT DIDN'T STOP him from marveling at the incredible versatility of the English language—at how, sometimes, a single word could have wildly unrelated meanings. A great many words were remarkable that way, but the word "chum" was the current object of his admiration. Sometimes it referred to an associate, but, at other times, it meant the blood and carcass parts thrown into the ocean to attract sharks. And then there were those exceptional circumstances, like right now, when it meant both at the same time. One word, two utterly different meanings, yet somehow the same. Normally, such an insight would've brought at least a smile, but tonight, it left him disappointed instead.

In the dim light of a half-moon, Joe sat on the starboard deck of Marty Truman's little cabin cruiser—the *Sea Dragon*—facing out over the dark Atlantic, one leg on either side of a rail post, to keep from falling overboard. With one hand, he dragged a garbage bag out over the side, and, with his other hand, he used a box cutter to slit the straining plastic. The penultimate serving of the former Marty Truman sluiced into the water below with a series of flat plopping sounds.

The irony of Marty's livelihood—loan sharking—wasn't lost on Joe. In fact, despite his melancholy mood, Joe wondered if the growing assembly of Marty's finned brethren would take a pass on consuming his remains, out of professional courtesy, or if their feeding would be all the more frenzied as they savored the rare delicacy of dining on one of their own.

Marty had been a longtime friend and a very profitable colleague, so it grieved Joe that things were ending this way. There was honor among thieves, as the old saying went, just not very much. And as old social mores eroded, there seemed to be less every day. But, in all the years Joe had known him, Marty had been utterly scrupulous in his financial dealings—head and shoulders above the rest—so it came as a surprise that he had allowed his greed to eclipse his better judgment. Marty had taken what wasn't his—a lot of what wasn't his—and if there was one sin in Joe's world that trumped every kind of relationship, it was stealing what belonged to someone smarter and meaner than you.

Most people thought of loan sharks as doing small, extortionate deals with mooks on the street, and there were plenty who did that, but there were also those who made big loans to sophisticated criminal enterprises that needed funding to take advantage of important opportunities. That had been Marty's field of expertise. He'd been a packager. Crooks had come to him with an idea, and Marty had found people with deep pockets willing to fund the idea in exchange for a hefty piece of the action.

Eight months earlier, a cargo thief had come to Marty looking for upfront money to obtain the specialized personnel and equipment required to take down a huge, very valuable shipment coming into the Port of Savannah. She'd also needed money to bribe the right people to get the stolen merchandise into bonded warehouses and, from there, finagled into legitimate commerce.

It had looked like a solid deal, so Joe and Charlie had loaned Marty just shy of four million bucks, which Marty had put together with some of his own money, and then he'd lent the whole shebang to the thief. After that, everything had ticked along as planned. The robbery had gone off without a hitch, the stolen goods were being sold off, the loan payments were coming in right on schedule, and Marty had been handing Joe and Charlie their piece. But, a week before Joe and Charlie had been supposed to receive their share of the balloon payment—the biggest part of the payoff that would close out the loan—the cargo thief had died from complications related to the birth of her third child.

When Marty had broken the news, he'd added that the thief had died *before* she'd made the final payment, which had meant that collecting was going to be difficult and time-consuming. But Joe and Charlie hadn't just fallen off the turnip truck. They knew a stalling tactic when they saw one, and they'd also gathered, from a stray remark overheard during a recent social event on the *Sea Dragon*, that Marty had had his eye on getting out of the business in the not too distant future.

Through a backchannel, Joe and Charlie had discovered that, contrary to Marty's claim, the balloon payment actually had been made. That, they'd known, had meant Marty had been trying to get them to sit still long enough for him to pull a vanishing act with his fair share and theirs. So, Joe and Charlie had played along, keeping an eye on their erstwhile friend and sometime business partner until they'd been sure he'd been in physical possession of their money and just about to disappear into the wind.

Earlier tonight, they had watched Marty load several pieces of luggage onto the *Sea Dragon*, at the Cumberland Island Marina on the St. Marys River, and then head out into the Atlantic. They had waited until he'd been clear of the near-shore traffic, then had come alongside him in their Zodiac inflatable, and, like pirates, they had climbed aboard and forced Marty to give up the cash—his and theirs. They'd also made him sign over the title to the boat, which they'd found stowed with other papers in a hidey-hole under the floor in the main cabin. After that, they'd hauled the Zodiac onto the deck and spent the next two hours down below, dismembering and bagging Marty for distribution to the fishes.

Joe turned at the sound of footsteps on the ladder and watched Charlie's head, then his shoulders and arms, then all the rest of him rise through the hatch, one rung at a time, as the big man made his way topside, muscling another bag of Marty in front of him.

"This is the last of it." The plastic made a wet kissing sound when Charlie dropped it onto the deck. "How we doing?" He leaned against the wheelhouse, cloaking himself in shadow.

"So far so good. But I'm still worried about trace evidence. No matter how much we scrub downstairs, there's bound to be something left. At some point, when people notice Marty's not around anymore, calls will be made and the police will start checking into everything, including this tub."

Charlie shook his head. "Who's gonna report him missing? Both of his exes are dead. He's got no kids that he knows of. No other friends to speak of. So, besides people looking to borrow money—and that ain't an everyday occurrence—who the hell's gonna be hounding the cops into snooping around for his sorry, light-fingered ass?"

"Just saying. Luminol is a terrible thing in the wrong hands. This whole boat will probably light up like a neon sign."

"And I'm just saying it's nothing we'll ever have to worry about. Before anybody even thinks about nosing around here, enough time will have passed to get the hull repainted, the deck totally sanded and refinished, and everything below pulled and refurbed good as new."

Joe noticed that Charlie hadn't said *they* would be doing all those things, only that there'd be enough time to—implying that Charlie might have ambitions to do them on his own. Joe realized he might be hearing more than Charlie was saying, but, truth be told, he hadn't been totally comfortable with Charlie over the last few months.

They were all getting older—except for Marty—so looking for a safe path out of such a hard-nosed business wouldn't be unexpected, but experience counseled that those closest to you were the likeliest to try to pick you off if they thought you were going soft. Which meant it wasn't entirely out of the question that Charlie might turn on him. The man had definitely been giving off a different vibe lately—the kind of thing Joe's instincts told him he could never afford to ignore.

Joe's natural cynicism kept him from being blinded by friendship, so he had seen the changes in Charlie early enough to come up with a plan to protect himself in the event his longtime comrade started to look threatening. And now he was glad he had, because as much as he hated to even allow the thought into his mind, this looked like the right moment to kick that plan into motion and retire Charlie right along with Marty. Better safe than sorry, or dead.

A noise from the darkness around the wheelhouse pulled Joe's thoughts back into the moment. He could see that Charlie was studying him.

As though he'd been reading Joe's mind, Charlie bent his right elbow, bringing his hand up to waist-level, his fingers curled around the grip of a gun-shaped mass pointing straight at Joe.

"Is that what I think it is?" Joe peered into the shadows, trying to figure out what Charlie was holding, his gaze toggling between Charlie's face and the dark thing aimed in his direction.

"Afraid so." Charlie's index finger tightened, blasting Joe with a cone of blinding light.

"Very funny." Joe's heart kicked into overdrive as his forearm went up to block the glare.

Charlie laughed and stepped away from the wheelhouse, directing the beam of his pistol-grip Streamlight out over the side of the boat where a half-dozen dorsal fins—big ones—zigzagged through the rust-colored slick spreading away from the hull.

Joe stared, mesmerized by the graceful deadly creatures.

"Let's dump the rest of this stuff," Charlie said. "So we can get the hell out of here."

Joe dragged the bag across the gunwale and held it out over the edge, then reached under it with the box cutter and ran the blade along the bottom. As the last of Marty Truman's mortal remains spilled out into the ocean, Charlie planted the sole of his size-fourteen foot against Joe's shoulder blade and pushed hard, spinning Joe around the rail post and out over the water.

Joe's eyes went wide and his hands clutched at the air as he tumbled into the seething swarm of sharks. Charlie focused his flashlight on the splash and watched as the water churned into a furious pink foam.

Almost instantly, Joe's head and shoulders were thrust upward, his hair plastered against his forehead, his arms flapping uselessly at the sleek gray beast that held him like a panicked albatross straining to reach escape velocity. Crimson froth spewed from his mouth as he surged sideways with grim animal purpose, pushing up a small bow wave along the line of his movement, causing Charlie to notice how much Joe resembled one of the little rubber duck targets that floated down the trough in a carnival shooting gallery. He aimed his Streamlight at Joe's head and snapped his wrist up a few times, pretending to squeeze off a series of shots, until Joe was finally dragged under.

"I'll take that stuffed shark," Charlie crowed, pointing off into the night, as though he were telling some grudgingly impressed carny which prize he wanted as a reward for his stunning display of marksmanship.

After watching the sharks for a few more minutes, Charlie stepped up to the helm and fired the engines. He was going to miss their outings on the *Sea Dragon*. The boat was getting a bit long in the tooth, and, even without having to deal with the mess below, a lot of work would've been needed to get it back into prime condition, but it had still been a great perch for howling at the moon over a lot of crazy years. With Joe's abrupt departure, though, keeping it now seemed like bad idea. No matter how many new playmates Charlie might bring onboard in the coming years, the *Dragon* would be forever freighted with the ugly memories of how Joe had left the party for the last time and how it might just as easily have been Charlie in the water with the sharks. He had no interest in cruising around on a floating reminder of that.

Charlie opened the throttle all the way and let the salt wind blow away the fatigue of a long night. After he put a couple of miles between himself and the sharks, he dropped back to idle, used a couple of bungies to secure the wheel onto a northward heading, and then went below. He pulled the covers off the engine compartment, unscrewed the caps on both fuel tanks, and then moved into one of the portside staterooms, where he assembled a crude igniter from the kitchen timer, wooden matches, and sandpaper he collected from the galley.

On his way topside, he taped the contraption to the table near the rear bulkhead, then closed the hatch so the gas fumes would continue building up. Moving quickly, Charlie tied the Zodiac's bow line to a deck cleat and slid the little craft into the water so it rode just below the starboard ladder, right alongside the wheelhouse, and then he went below one last time. The air, heavy with the smell of gasoline, was making him queasy. He set the timer for twenty minutes, grabbed the duffel they had stuffed the money into, and then scampered up onto deck. After easing the throttle forward a touch, he backed down the ladder into the inflatable and set himself adrift.

Once the *Sea Dragon* was about four hundred yards away, Charlie yanked the pull-cord and the Zodiac's motor roared to life. Absently, he babied the throttle, keeping pace with the larger boat while his mind wandered into a thicket of mawkish recollections about their jaunts down through the Keys and out to the Dry Tortugas. As he puzzled over these unexpectedly wistful thoughts, the *Dragon* erupted in a black-orange flash of splintering wood and fiberglass, and the *basso profundo whoomp* of the detonation sent a blast wave of hot air rushing over him.

Anxious to avoid falling debris, Charlie twisted the throttle all the way open and peeled away from the explosion, making a beeline for dry land.

Coming ashore at an actual dock would have been so much easier, but Charlie wanted to avoid the scrutiny that would open him to, so he beached the Zodiac among the barnacled pylons supporting an abandoned surfside restaurant, then dragged it into an unused utility shed. Home was three miles away, and hoofing it was the only way to get there without leaving a trail, but he was in fine shape, so after he wiped down the inflatable with a gas-soaked shop rag, he loped off into the darkness with the money-filled duffel strapped to his back.

Once he was home, Charlie gave himself a pat on the back for coming out on top, because things could easily have gone the other direction. But during his homeward trek, he realized he didn't feel the way he'd thought he would. The thrill of victory had quickly succumbed to a growing sense of listlessness and isolation. He and Joe had been partners for the better part of twenty years. And he and Joe and Marty had made a ton of money together. Sure, they had all been showing signs of wanting to find an easier row to hoe—always a dangerous maneuver in the life they had chosen—but the endgame had left him dissatisfied.

Having to waste Marty had been tough, but letting someone get away with ripping you off was suicidal—an invitation for other, more lethal individuals to try.

Doing Joe had been worse, even though Charlie was sure Joe had been only inches away from doing him. He'd seen the subtle change in Joe's face as they'd eyed each other on the boat—that knowing look that had said Joe had realized he'd been in danger and had needed to act fast. But Charlie had acted faster. Joe had left him no choice. Yet something wasn't right.

Maybe it was just the gruesome way Joe had died. A small part of Charlie wondered if that had been absolutely necessary, but the biggest part of him insisted that friends who plotted to betray surely deserved the worst.

Or was it that bit with the flashlight that was bothering him? Acting like he was shooting toy targets at the county fair while his lifelong business partner was being eaten alive? What kind of person reacted that way to the grisly death of a close companion—even a companion who deserved to die? The kind of person who needed to stay armored against the dangers that feeling squeamish would leave him vulnerable to, that was who. So why, he asked, did he now feel so odd about the whole thing?

Charlie caught sight of himself in the mirror over the console table in his foyer, and he didn't like the weak brooding spirit he saw lurking in the lines of his face. *Enough of this sappy, maudlin jibbering,* he thought, staring himself in the eye. If he kept on like this, it wouldn't be long before he wound up practicing mindfulness, or lying on some shrink's couch, trying to get in touch with his feelings. *Just fix yourself a nice big drink,* he told himself. *And count your money. You earned it.*

But he wasn't in the mood. The rucksack full of cash, slumped against the wall by the front door, bore silent witness to the fact that the scales of his life were now out of kilter in a way he didn't understand.

And then it hit him. Marty and Joe had been dangerous but necessary, and now they were gone. Their very nature had given him something. His entire life required that he be able to coexist with forces that could kill him and would do so at the very first moment it seemed appropriate. How strange he'd never noticed this before. Suddenly, he was like the lion tamer with no lion, or the snake charmer with no snake—not just alone, but undefined. Truly alone.

Except that his mind was crowded with memories of Joe and Marty—who they were and the purpose they'd served. Until last night, killing had been a simple matter of survival, so he hadn't anticipated that the deaths of Joe and Marty would show him anything new—and certainly not anything about himself. Yet they had.

Charlie smiled, grateful for this gift of insight from his late friends. Rebalancing his life would be much easier now. There were other Joes and Martys out there. He would just have to find them. Until then, he'd be alone with his memories… and a huge pile of money. He winked at his reflection in the mirror, then headed for the liquor cabinet.

The bottle of bourbon Joe had brought over to celebrate a construction scam they'd pulled off was still half-full. Charlie poured an inch of the mellow amber fluid into a highball glass, then raised a toast in honor of his friends—gone for good, but with him forever.

HOLLIS GILLESPIE

COVID Cover Letters

[During the COVID-19 Quarantine and subsequent demolition of my jobs in the journalism and travel industries, these are actual cover letters I wrote to accompany my applications in response to job alerts from *Indeed.com* (after Ivanka Trump aimed her "Find Something New" campaign at people like me, who make up the historical number of America's formerly gainfully employed people).]

Cover Letter: Chocolate Quality and Compliance Manager for Rocky Mountain Chocolates in Durango, CO.

I saw your job posting on Indeed.com, and, oh my GOD, you could scan the universe like a human hair trap and not find anyone better suited to be your chocolate-quality manager than me. I have lived in Zurich, Switzerland, where the chocolate tastes like a sunrise on your tongue. And I have lived in a trailer two miles north of Tijuana, Mexico, where the chocolate tastes like it's made from melted dump-truck tires. Suffice it to say I know good chocolate, and I know bad chocolate, and will happily devour them both as my duty to you.

I used to be a writer and magazine columnist, but what was left of my industry after it got obliterated by a bunch of Millennials banging out "blogs" for free in their mother's basement was washed down the drain during the COVID shutdown. So hence the offer of my service to you. (You're welcome!) My expert chocolate-checking process requires a bite at the beginning of each batch, and one at the end. And if it's a batch of chocolate bunnies, I will need to bite off the ears and tails of the first forty or so before I'll bestow my approval and wave the rest through.

Along with my sommelier-like expertise in chocolate quality assurance, I offer my considerable skills in chocolate manufacturing, which consists of having watched, exactly eleven hundred times, that *I Love Lucy* episode in which Lucy and Ethel try to work the conveyor belt at the chocolate factory and end up stuffing their bras with bon bons because the belt was going too fast. But that will never happen with me. Those two only stuffed their bras because they ran out of room in their mouths. My mouth, I assure you, will never run out of room for chocolate.

In addition, I am very organized (even without medication), good at pointing out things in people's teeth, tri-lingual (I can say, "Dang, this good-ass chocolate needs more macadamia nuts!" in Spanish, German and English), talented at fork-lift driving (probably), picking raisins out of bridge mix, disposing of used needles, and basket weaving. I will happily relocate to Durango, CO, from the inner city of Atlanta, where my neighbors are in the habit of abandoning old mattresses in my back yard. Please hire me.

Sincerely,
Hollis Gillespie

Cover Letter: Dispensary Cannabis Store Manager, Presented by Regis HR Group in Miami, FL.

Hello, I saw your job posting on Indeed.com, and I was born to do this job. I mean, what a WONDERFUL reason to wake up every morning. The only job better than this on the scale of awesome jobs might, only just possibly, be as a subject of a science experiment in which my dopamine is measured after spending a day kissing Corgi puppies.

Plus, I would NEVER over-indulge in your store product. I haven't smoked pot since the late '70s, and between you and me I don't think it was even really pot. It was just a bag of sticks and seeds my friends and I paid five bucks for, and none of us knew how to roll a joint. Our joint was as tight and compact as a plastic sack of circus peanuts. When I took a hit I might as well have been sucking fumes from a burning sewage pipe. I didn't get high but pretended I did by staring blankly, laughing a lot and eating an entire bag of Nicaraguan pig rinds—pretty much my normal behavior so I will FIT RIGHT IN at your cannabis dispensary!

I see there are certain medical licenses you require, such as certifications in being a physician's assistant, RN, or pharmacist, but I was a flight attendant for 20 years, during which time I completed annual recertification training in such areas as Bringing People Back from the Dead (sometimes referred to as CPR), Household Heart Surgery (i.e. defibrillator-use know-how), Intense Anger-Issue Psychotherapy (terrorism negotiation), Being an Orderly to the Insane (or as we in the industry call it, "passenger service"), High-Level Defense Security Maneuvers (tackling drunks before they break into the cockpit) and Heroism (heroism). Surely these skills fill those requirements.

I'm also good at working cash registers, doing deep knee bends, saving albino baby rhinos, speaking Spanish, dodging bullets, amateur ventriloquism, and bee keeping (also amateur). I'm happy to relocate, seeing as I now live in the inner city of Atlanta, where, according to the Georgia sex-offender registry, my house is currently surrounded by marauding miscreants. Please hire me.

Sincerely,
Hollis Gillespie

Cover Letter: Administrative Assistant for a Mountain Guide Company in Skagway, AK.

I saw your job posting on Indeed.com, and oh my GOD, I love Skagway, I love Alaska and this job sounds like the epicenter of all things awesome in the universe. I have a lot of administrative experience, I'm a genius at organization (my bathroom cabinet alone should be featured in magazines), I'm energetic (just today I successfully dove clear of a bus barreling through a crosswalk) and a people person (which in resume-speak means I'm patient with idiots). I'm also a foreign-language interpreter—I can say, "Holy Hell THAT'S A MOOSE!" in German, Spanish and English.

To work in Skagway for Alaskan Mountain Guides I would seriously fall over backwards and foam at the mouth in gratitude. I'm pretty sure the pay is terrible, but who cares? The job is in SKAGWAY! For a MOUNTAIN GUIDE company! I, for one, cannot RESIST towns founded by bootleggers and whores! They are the best, most interesting, most colorful places on the planet. Please let me work for you! PLEASE! I live in Atlanta now, and I'm dying (probably literally) to get out of here. Yesterday somebody dumped a bunch of masticated chicken bones on my driveway. Just say the word and I'll appear like a Leprechaun on your doorstep! At the ready to assist administration. Just tell me when to start.

Sincerely,
Hollis Gillespie

Cover Letter: "Whale Watcher Supervisor" in Oahu, HI.

Hello, I saw your job posting on Indeed.com. First, wow, this is the first I've ever even HEARD of a "whale watcher supervisor," but I thoroughly believe it is definitely, without a doubt, absolutely probably the best job in the history of the universe. Does the whale-watcher supervisor get to have whale-watcher subordinates? Like lower-level whale watchers I'd get to boss around and tell things like, "Look over there! Did you see that WHALE?!?!?! IT WAS AN AWESOME WHALE! Next time make sure you see it or I'll write you a stern reprimand." Because if so I'd be good at that. I also speak three languages. I can say, "JESUS GOD THAT'S A DAMN WHALE!" in English, Spanish and German. Germans would especially be amazed by whales. They don't have whales in Germany. In fact, if it's a slow whale day, I could point out a porpoise and say it's a whale and they would not know the difference, trust me.

I have never been a professional whale watcher, but I tried it as an amateur once and proved to have a knack. Also, I used to be a flight attendant, which I know is almost the opposite of being a whale watcher because I worked three miles in the sky where there are hardly, if any, whales. But I did undergo safety re-certification training every year for 20 years, during which I had to prove I could save people's lives by, among other things, performing CPR, putting out fires, operating a defibrillator, Heimlich maneuvering people (my favorite), stabbing people with epi pens (second favorite), secretly sedating babies behind their mothers' backs (not really), negotiating with terrorists (seriously), disarming bombs (again seriously), evacuating passengers and surviving plane wrecks by outrunning the ball of fire barreling through the fuselage.

Believe me, I am definitely the person you want watching your whales. I can also whistle like a dockworker, with two fingers. I don't know if this talent is important unless whales come when you whistle, but you never know; they're smart creatures. Whistling also gets people's attention, especially if the ship is full of selfie-obsessed tourists too busy doing duck lips to watch the ocean where the whales are. That there is a valuable skill. I'm also good at organizing and scheduling shifts, mainly because if anyone called in sick or had an emergency I'd cover their shift myself because OH MY GOD who wouldn't want to watch whales every day of their life? Also, I do not get seasick. I've got a gut like a galvanized drum.

I am also very good at NOT falling overboard. You would not believe how good I am at that. It's only happened, at the most,

MAYBE 11 times, but every single time it was on a booze cruise in Key West, where falling overboard is almost mandatory, so that doesn't count. Also I'm good at diffusing tense situations, changing flat tires, making people laugh, pulling on ropes and hammering things. All attributes that make for an astounding Whale Watch Supervisor. Thank you for your time, consideration, and when do I start?

Sincerely,
Hollis Gillespie

Cover Letter: Assistant Manager Position, Grand Canyon Association.

I saw your job posting on Indeed.com. First, I'd be the best assistant manager of the Grand Canyon that ever existed in the history of the universe. I've been there many times, starting when I was 13 and my parents kept calling the place "The Big Ditch." I still have a picture of them at the scenic point, hugging each other. That is saying a lot, because they did not stay married much longer after that.

As assistant manager of the Grand Canyon, I assume I will be in charge of the donkeys that deliver people up and down the canyon switchbacks, and I very much look forward to that. When I was a kid I was too afraid to ride a donkey to the bottom of the canyon but today nothing scares me. I'm not brave, just old. When you're old, dying by donkey-back is AWESOME! Whereas if you're young it's just tragic.

Speaking of bucket lists, I already hiked the Grand Canyon in junior college on a field trip with my Geology class, which is when I learned the word "stratified." I use it a lot still and will continue to use as Assistant Manager of the Grand Canyon, such as in, "Look here at this chart of stratified soil samples embedded with fish fossils" and such. I also learned a number of stupid reasons people die in the Grand Canyon. Like how campers get up to pee at night with no light and end up walking right off the edge, or how hikers sit down too close to the brink and their heavy backpacks simply pull them right off the edge, or how tourists take pictures of their spouses against the scenery of the canyon and keep telling them, "Just one more step back," until the poor spouse just back-steps right off the edge. Personally, I'd rather die by donkey-back ("The Donkey Walked Her Right Off the Edge"), but death by Grand Canyon dumb-assery would probably fall a good fourth on my list. As Assistant Manager of the Grand Canyon, I will keep good track of all the easily avoided deaths with prominently placed signs that read, "24 [or however many number of] Dumb-Ass Death-Free Days!" and whatnot to encourage canyon-place safety.

I see that heavy lifting is a desired qualification. I'm good at that. My ex-husband is a former professional linebacker and I carried his ass for 11 years. I'm also trilingual. I can say, "Watch out for that falling donkey!" in German, Spanish and English. I'm also good at inflating air mattresses, amateur cricket farming, cobbling shoes, intending to donate to good causes, defending underdogs, collecting antique proctology tools, and dentistry (also amateur). I look forward to your response.

Sincerely,
Hollis Gillespie

Cover Letter: Bull-Semen Extractor Intern, World West Sire Services, Joliet, MT.

Hello, I saw your job posting on Indeed.com. Right off the bat I want to emphasize I would be the best bull-semen extractor intern you ever saw. I can't say I've had a lot of contact with bovine genitals, but I'm a very enthusiastic and punctual person. I would show up on time every time you needed me to assist in extracting the best bull semen. Plus, I figure bull genitals function the same as most mammalian male genitals, which is to say the less experienced the extractor the (probably) better. I mean, most bulls aren't gonna want a semen extractor who's been extracting semen indiscriminately all over town, all jaded and worn out, probably not wearing any gloves or remembering any names and faces. They'd likely be more responsive to a fresh first-timer like me. I could bat my eyes coyly and pretend to be all agog over the "size of that thing" and such.

I noticed in the job description that there was a lot of reference to "product packing," and, while I'm unsure of how bull semen would be packaged, but it seems to me it's already perfectly packaged right there in the bull balls. Have you considered keeping the sperm in there? See, instead of extracting the semen and packaging it, you could just walk the bull over to where you want the semen to be. I know it would be counter-intuitive to the "extractor" part of the job title, but that is the kind of innovative thinking you can expect from me as your bull-semen extractor intern. I just have one question: As the bull-semen extractor intern, would my duties include cuddling afterward? Or is that reserved for the senior semen-extractor staff?

My other talents include gluing things, making blender-based meals, re-chroming old car fenders, driving on sidewalks, locating lost wallets, spackling drywall, and amateur anesthesia. I would love to relocate from Atlanta, which is suffering a serious deficiency of virile bulls, to Montana, where, evidently, bull balls are so bursting with semen they need assistants to catch and package it all. I look forward to your response.

Sincerely,
Hollis Gillespie

Cover Letter: Highly Educated Childcare Provider at Educated Nannies in Los Angeles, CA.

I'm responding to your job posting on Indeed.com looking for a polished, super-educated professional nanny to take care of your toddlers. First, I'd be the best nanny in the history of the galaxy.

I don't have any actual professional child-care experience, but I'm overly educated and I have given actual birth to an actual human and raised that human girl child to be a badass college student who, despite my pleadings, won't move out of the country with me to escape the totalitarian regime that is the Trump administration. Said girl child insists on staying in the US and fighting for her rights. I raised her that way but at the same time when I was raising her I didn't really expect there to be such a battle for her to fight, and didn't really expect her to take my standby instruction, "Don't be shy, kick 'em in the balls," so much to heart, but she did and I'm stuck supporting her here rather than getting a place in, say, Portugal, which I hear is a good outpost to ride out political unrest.

If you hire me as your nanny, I will teach your toddlers how to, among other things, break free of zip-tie handcuffs, which is practical knowledge right there. I'm really generous with this knowledge. Back when my girl had sleepovers at our house during middle school, parents would call the next morning to inquire as to why I returned their kids with ligature marks on their wrists and ankles. "You're welcome," I told them. To this day none of these kids have been successfully kidnapped and murdered. I can also teach your toddlers how to escape a car trunk. Ask my girl, who I locked into a car trunk when she was seven and yelled instructions at her from the outside on how to look for the glow-in-the-dark handle to release the boot— or if, God forbid, there was no glow-in-the-dark handle, in which case she should look for the car jack and jack her ass out of there.

Super practical knowledge there. I can totally attest, because my girl went and became a young adult who hardly needs me anymore, which I guess is the point, right? Though I've threatened to become a cafeteria lady at her college commissary with the goal of embarrassing her every day with loud exclamations like, "Darling! I think my vaginal mesh is defective!" she has thwarted that threat with a counter-threat to get engaged to a Trump-supporting trailer dweller who lives with a decrepit roommate referred to as "Uncle Touchy" by area kids. So in the end I am left with no outlet for all my maternal maxi-pad sappiness. A huge plus for you!

And you're also in luck because I also see that you are looking for someone who is multi-lingual. I'm an officially international airline-qualified foreign-language interpreter, and I can say, "Get away from that Axe-Wielding, Blood-Covered Circus Clown!" in German, Spanish and English (which, arguably, is an actual language). I'm also good at pickle brining, butterfly farming, de-escalating family infighting, drinking wine and profusely complimenting people, amateur taxidermy, alligator wrestling (also amateur) and taste-testing artisan tequila. Let me know when I can start.

Sincerely,
Hollis Gillespie

LAURETTA HANNON

'Twixt & 'Tween

—quarantining and racial conflicts conjure up some singular memories

THERE'S NO OTHER WAY TO SAY IT: MY MOTHER WAS A BLACK supremacist. Trouble is, she was white. Or *was* she?

When Mama worked in a nursing home, her favorite resident was Miss Bessie. First thing every morning, she would visit with her friend, who happened to be ninety-four and African-American. Before Mama would leave, they'd exchange I-Love-Yous.

One day, Miss Bessie asked her to lean in close because she had a secret to tell. As Mama put her ear in front of Miss Bessie's lips, the ancient one whispered, "I *hate* all white folks."

"Now wait a minute," Mama said. "Somethin's bad wrong with this picture, Miss Bessie. I'm white, and you don't hate me."

Silence… Miss Bessie took Mama's arm. Squinting hard at the arm, she rubbed the outside of it, flipped it over, and did the same thing to the inside. After careful scrutiny, she arrived at her finding.

"Sybil, you ain't white, and you ain't black. You're somewhere 'twixt and 'tween."

Miss Bessie was right on the mark. Despite coming up in a racist family and environment, Mama never looked down on black folks. In fact, she looked up, *way* up. She decided that African Americans were more advanced and generally superior because of what they'd endured… and that extra respect and reverence were deserved. This was instilled in me early.

Our views were always clashing with the notions of others in 1970s Georgia. I had friends in grade school whose dogs barked only at black people. The N-word rolled off the forked tongues of Mama's hick relatives like it was just another word. During our stint in her hometown, I was reprimanded for playing with the black kids on the playground. When my kindergarten mates would sing, "Eeny, meeny, miny, moe—catch a (N-word) by the toe," I'd sing over them, belting out, "Catch a *tiger* by the toe!" When a guest in our home referred to Brazil nuts as "(N-word) toes," Mama gave him a lashing that only a five-foot-tall package of ignited human dynamite could unleash.

"We do not use that word in this house!" she roared, flames flashing in her eyes. "*Do you hear me?!*"

Sidney Poitier was her favorite actor. She did a truly dreadful impression of him delivering his famous line from the film *In the Heat of the Night*.

Here's the dialogue between the white police chief, played by Rod Steiger, and Virgil Tibbs, Poitier's character:

CHIEF GILLESPIE (Steiger): *Well, you're pretty sure of yourself, ain't you, Virgil. Virgil, that's a funny name for a (N-word) boy to come from Philadelphia! What do they call you up there?*

VIRGIL (Poitier): *They call me* Mister Tibbs!

The line marks a turning point in the movie as Poitier's character asserts his pride, self-respect, and defiance. He takes his stand. Mama liked that in people, especially when they were stickin' it to The Man.

She never wavered in her support of those who possessed the most melanin. Regardless of the competition or situation, Mama would be on the side of the African American contestant, player, prosecutor, defendant, or entertainer. When NFL Hall-of-Famer Jerry Rice was on *Dancing with the Stars*, she smelled a conspiracy right from the start. Convinced that the elder white judge was prejudiced against him, she voted over a hundred times for "her Jerry."

"It's plain as day that that white man has it in for my Jerry. Shoot, even Stevie Wonder could see that, Retta!"

I watched the show to judge for myself. It didn't go over well when I made the blasphemous remark that Jerry didn't appear to be the strongest dancer on the show.

People outside the rural South have no idea of the complexity of our perspectives and relationships. Would you expect a scantily educated, dirt-poor woman of Mama's era to have this mindset? Have you seen it depicted in a movie yet?

As Sybil's understudy, I was passionate about racial concerns and perceived things through the filter she imparted. I've gone out of my way to support black businesses. In high school, I recited Dr. Martin Luther King, Jr.'s words over the intercom during Black History Month. I was among the first white people to march in the King Parade at the University of Georgia, despite the hell I caught from both races. Dr. King was my pastor for years of Sundays as I listened to his speeches and sermons broadcast on the university radio station. I took every Civil Rights History course offered. I wasn't trying to be a righteous babe; it was just how I was brought up.

In college, I shared a one-bedroom apartment with an African-American girl and saw how clerks would follow her around in stores but not give me a second look. I should have stolen them blind and split the loot with her. We'd go through small-town squares on our occasional drives home from college. These journeys would prompt stares from people on the street. Once, we passed a subdivision named for a fellow with the surname of "White." His initials were printed in tiny script on the subdivision sign so that at a glance it read: WHITE SUBDIVISION. My roommate said, "That had *better* be someone's name." I nodded, and we laughed for a mile. (As a side note, this girl is a talented artist who later sold a painting to Mr. Sidney Poitier Himself.)

Mama's teachings prepared me for work that would come later—and caused a lot of internal confusion. For almost 20 years, I was the lone white senior administrator at predominately African-American colleges. I was one of a handful of Caucasian women out of hundreds of staff members.

Immersion in a different culture was eye-opening and harsh at times. I became aware of subtle biases I harbored. Worst of all, it showed me that African Americans are not superior, just equal. The coldest shock was witnessing the wide and penetrating disdain that exists toward folks who look like me. James Baldwin's words came to mind: "To be a Negro in this country and to be relatively conscious is to be in a rage almost all the time."

I cannot condemn that, either, because I don't know jack shit about the African-American experience. I'm still listening, asking, and learning. I am not an Enlightened Caucasian and am certainly not woke. Anyone who thinks she is woke is likely the one most asleep at the wheel.

Something I did understand a bit better was the psychological effect of being in a minority disparaged by the majority. After hearing about two longstanding putdowns of white folks—that we're greasy and smell like wet dogs—I became worried that my hair was oily and my deodorant wasn't enough. I stashed clinical-strength antiperspirant under my desk and inspected my hair daily. Ridiculous, I know, but real nonetheless. Imagine the cumulative effect this would have over generations and several hundred years. And add slavery. Ancestors in chains, bought and sold. An identity you can't even trace or name.

Although it was painful to lose the belief in black supremacy, I think some essence of Mama's theory holds true. Consider the person of Hank Thomas, a board member at one of my colleges. He was one of the original thirteen Freedom Riders. Arrested 22 times for the cause of civil rights. Survivor of the infamous bus firebombing in Anniston, Alabama, in 1961. Endurer of beatings by authorities and klansmen who had just gotten out of church and brought their children to the beating. Leader of the singing among the inmates at the notorious Parchman State Prison Farm (where the day's food was two pieces of bread and a cup of water). Medic and Purple Heart recipient in the Vietnam War. After Vietnam, he became an incredibly astute entrepreneur who went on to build a business empire. One of the most successful in the nation. He said it's all about determination and not making excuses. He said it was a twelve-year-old white girl who brought him water as he barely escaped the fiery bus. She was the only one who rendered aid. He said that of the thirteen Freedom Riders, seven were African-American and six were Caucasian (two of whom were Holocaust survivors). He spared no details of the gruesome hatred and violence he encountered. But he also sang of the goodness of all people. He said not to linger too long in the past, but to focus on the vast opportunities his generation made possible. In this season of panic porn and cancel culture, we are not hearing about heroes like Hank Thomas.

Mama had a hero, too. A vivacious bisexual musician from just up the road in Macon, Georgia. The undisputed architect of rock-n-roll and the "beauty on duty": Little Richard Penniman. Mama was thirteen when her church burned her Little Richard records. Devil music. Sex. Race mixing. I've wondered how this moment affected her. Perhaps it made her more resolute in her convictions. It could explain why she wore those convictions like a cement suit with cinder-block shoes. Mama would not be moved, cracked, or persuaded.

When she decided that we needed a lift, she'd put on the Little Richard singles, and we'd have wild "dance parties" in our little apartment by the railroad tracks. Just Mama and me. We'd imitate his hair-on-fire expressions and frenetic piano pounding. We'd holler "A-wop-bop-a-loo-bop-a-wop-bam-boom!" and then rear back our heads—hootin' and howlin'—whirling 'round and 'round until collapsing on the worn-out sofa. Emptied of our troubles—for a while, at least.

It was bad enough that Bill Withers died during the pandemic, but Little Richard, too? He went to the Land of Limitless Tutti Frutti on Mother's Day weekend.

MY LITTLE RICHARD STORY

Mama detested it when I'd call her while I was driving. She'd say, "Call me back when you're not on the road! It's too dangerous to talk and drive!" Then she'd hang up without even a goodbye. One day in 2003, I phoned her from the car. As she was preparing to disconnect the call, I squeezed in these words: "Stop! I have a Little Richard story!"

Suddenly, the air shifted. The birds fell silent. Instead of the familiar dial tone, I heard this: "Little Richard?! Well, Retta, *do tell.*"

Here's how it went. I was at S&S Cafeteria in Southwest Atlanta for lunch. The place was all a-twitter because Little Richard had been in the night before. I was a regular at S&S, so a gaggle of servers came to my booth to fill me in.

Me: *What was he doing in here?*

They: *He was eating before getting his hair did for his concert at Chastain Park. He always gets his hair did at the salon next door (appropriately named "Talk of the Town" salon).*

Me: *Why does he go there for his hair?*

They: *Aww, don't you know?! 'Cause they's old sissies in there.*

This was said matter-of-factly without a speck of negativity.

DON'T LOCK THE DOORS

Years back, I was approaching a stop sign in a notoriously sketchy Atlanta neighborhood. My friend, who is African-American, was with me. Some "gentlemen" (picture Dave Chapelle's crackhead character) and "working ladies" were standing in the street at the stop sign. My friend said, "Lock the doors!"

I said, "Nope, that's disrespectful and tells those folks I'm scared that they will do something bad—and I'm not scared, and I refuse to assume the worst. How can I love them if I'm afraid of them?" My friend just shook her head and said, "Okay, then… but you're crazy and putting us at risk. I'm locking *my* door."

That kind of scene played out hundreds of times during my tenure in Southwest Atlanta. Concerned colleagues uttered the same mantra: "Hannon, you're making yourself vulnerable. Don't do that. Don't go there by yourself. Don't leave yourself open."

I know I'm being vulnerable. That's the point. It's on purpose. I admit that I've taken some unnecessary risks, but mindful vulnerability over fear has never failed me, especially when I held the position of College Conduct Officer.

In this role, I dealt with students, mostly African-American men, who had done something to get in trouble, from mild infractions such as cheating all the way to serious assaults, major drug dealing with an AK-47 on campus, and so forth.

One time, a student exploded in a fury outside the Financial Aid office. Campus police were summoned. He was screaming, thrashing about, and hurling threats. He was brought to my office.

The officers wanted me to give them permission to take him straight to jail. Here was this 6'4" figure with dreadlocks down to his waist. Tattoos covered his face and neck. He was ready to pounce, and I was his target. Him python, me bunny rabbit. I was even wearing a diaphanous blouse and pearls.

I told the officers that I would meet with the student alone in my office. I further instructed them to close my door on the way out and said that they could wait outside. They thought I was asking for terrible trouble.

Still sitting behind my desk, I looked into the student's eyes and saw raw pain. He lunged across the desk and yelled, "I'm about to go *black* on your ass, lady!"

I leaned back in a relaxed manner, clutched my pearls, and said, "Do I look worried to you?"

At that moment, he was utterly disarmed. He convulsed into tears. I sat beside him and *listened*. For a good while. He described the pressures he was under, and I understood his desperation.

Two hours later, we emerged from my office. The police officers were aghast as the student and I hugged—not a safe, sideways hug, but a *real* hug. "What consequence are you going to issue in this case?" asked the officer. "Can we take him to jail now?"

"No, you may not. He has to get to class."

Mama liked this story even better than the one about Little Richard.

NICKI SALCEDO

COVID-19 *Sweet* 16

O N THE DAY YOU WERE BORN, I THOUGHT THE WORLD WAS coming to an end. I couldn't breathe. It wasn't pain I felt, but pressure. I believed you wanted to stay with me a little longer. You refused to be born.

In the months before your birth, you floated the wrong way in my womb. They told me you were breach. Your father placed a flashlight on the underside of my belly. You were a fish who moved toward the light. He would speak to you like my skin was a mere curtain. You twisted to hear his sound.

I first suspected that I was pregnant in July. In New York. I'd had high tea at the Plaza Hotel. It is a favorite memory, and now, when I think about it, I know that you were there inside of me. A little lima bean. I thought it was the city lights and rush that made me dizzy, but it was you. All these years later, when I see you drink a cup of tea, it feels like proof that you are mine.

Now you are sixteen.

I tried to write you a letter for your birthday. It has taken me months to find the words. How could we celebrate our despair? And worse, how could we explain that we weren't in despair at all? How could we wallow in our moments of happiness? Happiness and quiet.

If I had made a birthday card, it would have read:

Boredom, disappointment, relief, lonely isolation, rest, patience, worry, fatigue, gratitude.

Happy COVID-19 Sweet Sixteen!

I didn't write that. I tried to write again. I know now that the world is always coming to an end. Not just on the day that you were born, when I knew that I would ruin you. Every day is the end of the world. It doesn't matter what we were supposed to do this year. I know so many moms, friends that I love, who would do anything for one more birthday with their child who is now gone. While you ate birthday cake, I felt the ghosts of children watching us. Children who never lived to be six years old, twenty-five years old, fifty years old.

Here you are. Sweet Sixteen.

You've probably never heard the phrase "sweet sixteen and never been kissed." It seems so archaic. Why would anyone say that now? By the time I was your age, I had been kissed. But just barely. The week before my birthday, a boy at school grabbed me in the hallway and stole a kiss. If you had asked me then, I would've told you he was nice. I would've told you I liked him. If you ask me today, I will tell you the truth. He kissed me on a dare, and he never spoke to me again.

I turned sixteen feeling sad. I turned sixteen feeling happy. I vowed then to make every birthday afterward a great birthday. I love all my birthdays. The ones I spent at elementary school curriculum night. The birthdays alone in strange cities. The six months before and after my birthday, when I celebrate for no good reason other than I can. Please remember to celebrate your half-birthday.

You will be sweet every day of your life. I hope you make a plan for your Sweet Twenty-Seventh birthday. I want you to have a big party for your Sweet Sixty-First birthday. For your seventeenth birthday, I suggest we have no plan.

For these recent months, we have been alone as a family. I have shown you old *Twilight Zone* episodes about the consequences of isolation. We have watched all my favorite disaster movies. Creepy cabin-in-the-woods movies. We watched them. Creepy aliens invade the Earth. We watched those movies, too. This week, we turned to murder mysteries. *Knives Out, Rear Window, Dial M for Murder,* and *Psycho.* I'm still trying to ruin you after all. The world is terrible and frightening and filled with death. It is also filled with laughter and hope. We can't be afraid of any of these things.

On your sixteenth birthday, you asked if you could make your own cake. You made vanilla cupcakes from scratch. They were crumbly and sweet like life. Friends and family and teachers sent you videos with funny birthday messages. I realized I don't know all of your friends. I want to thank them for sending messages from the great beyond, down the block, and two houses over. There were songs and dances and smiling faces. None of you will be the same after this.

Should I tell you that you were never going to be the same anyway?

I won't tell you that. Stay the same. Stay sweet. I love you. Happy birthday.

AMY COX

FOXTROT 878

TRANSMISSION: FOXTROT 878
Intercepted 14May2020
Translated by SPC K Rodriguez
FT MEADE, MD

ATTENTION: "*Orion*," Third Governor of Virgo Cluster
Greetings from "*Moses*," Second Lieutenant, Gamma Division.

Firstly, sir, I would like to thank you for the opportunity you have given to me in following up on the field report of our initial scout, "*Joshua.*" Joshua has proven to be a valuable and willing comrade, and I commend him for his efforts in initiating contact on the Milky Way Gamma satellite, Earth. I had a part in Joshua's training not long ago and took note of his eagerness to assist in our movement. Dominion of the neighboring lower-density galaxy regions has been a slow process for us, but it is finally approaching fruition. Obtainment of the Gamma satellite and its unique flora of elements and resources is closer now than it has ever been. That is why, Orion, I feel it is of the highest importance that we obtain accurate intelligence about the inhabitants of the Gamma planet so that our plan of attack is efficient and foolproof.

As you know, Joshua arrived on site 25Aug2019 and departed 25Jan2020. Upon my arrival on 25Mar2020, I established a permanent base in the planet's upper mantle as per our plan and began following protocol for acquisition and eventual domination. However, I am grieved to report to you that complications have arisen in our agenda. Joshua's initial reports and baseline data, although thorough, have proved inaccurate in almost every domain. This report will attempt to address and correct the discrepancies in Joshua's records, formed by my observations of the current race of inhabitants and their activities and resources. Based on this new information, I will be pleased to offer my conclusions and recommendations on how to proceed with the Gamma (Earth) Project.

To begin with, I must point out the most pronounced error, which I discovered on my very first visit into a typical community setting. Joshua, after spending half a solar orbit on this satellite, failed to detect the presence of another stalker: Coronavirus. Commonly known on this planet as "COVID," this biological creeper presents as a virus and attaches to the human species individually. I cannot say that this strategy is very effective, as there is no stealth factor to speak of. The human scientists and medical professionals spread messages daily about how to avoid the virus. COVID appears highly contagious, but is relatively well managed by the population as a whole. I predict they will overcome the initial attack very well and eliminate the threat altogether in a few years' time. This virus could not have been the brainchild of one of the leading minds in the cosmos. If I had a guess, I would suspect this is the work of Cetus from the Perseus Cluster. I attended university with him, and he always was an impulsive and shortsighted fellow. At first, I viewed the presence of COVID as an opportunity. Acquisition of an entire planet is certainly simpler when the populace is distracted and weakened by another intruder, even if that intruder is elementary and inferior. Alas, it is not that simple, Orion. Despite the distraction of this paltry disturbance, I now know there are gaps in our understanding of Gamma's inhabitants. Joshua's reports simply reaffirm every stereotype our sources have created for Earth's most recent millennial solar revolutions. My findings are in stark contrast to Joshua's, and I will outline that evidence briefly.

I first will address Joshua's erroneous and misleading accounts in the area of economics. Joshua's statements about the location and function of many industries suggest thriving retail and restaurant businesses on most continents. However, I observe in my clandestine visits *in vivo* that most businesses only appear to be functioning normally. They maintain power and water services, and their outside signage suggests a regularly functioning place of enterprise. In actuality, most of these establishments are closed to customers and are visited only by managers who, curiously, pay former employees as though they are working and spend the day cleaning their facilities with great vigor, while doors remain locked to clientele. I have no idea how such practices support the current economic system, and I recommend further research into this area. Perhaps the Gamma residents have discovered an alternative theory of economics from which we can glean useful and updated methods.

I am particularly shocked at Joshua's blunder in emphasizing the importance of restaurants, cafés, and coffee shops in both the economic and social realms of communities. We all know that our establishment of the Seattle Coffee Experiment has been wildly successful and has resulted in a plethora of intelligence. Since its inception in the early 1970s, the retail coffee chain has grown in popularity with Gamma residents to the point that we can boast infiltration to locations throughout the planet. The coffee project, staffed mainly by our entry-level informants, has steadily reported gains in the past decade, which supported the implementation of our level-two strategy, home assault. The popular in-home electronic personal assistants, as you know, provide a more thorough and personal layer to intelligence gathering for our team. Together with the home personal assistants, we have considered the Coffee Experiment to be successful to an exceptional degree for both data gathering and disseminating our propaganda.

The point I am making is this: it seems people do not visit restaurants with great frequency and that restaurants do not drive economic spending nearly as much as Joshua reported. That would explain why their doors are closed and they maintain only a skeleton staff. I cannot come to any conclusion other than the likelihood that Joshua has contrived data regarding both the popularity of the coffee project and the information obtained from resident work devices at store locations. It is true that the coffee shops enjoy global tenancy, but I surmise that their reported level of public esteem is but a ruse. The stores are closed, sir. They are deserted. The image of plentiful consumers working on laptops while sipping expensive bean roast infusions is false, though it disappoints me to say it. My first recommendation is to discard the nearly fifty years of data obtained in the highly regarded coffee project in favor of an alternative means of gathering consistent and accurate information about this species. My recommendation will likely be studying a phenomenon called "social media," which lately has enjoyed steady growth and popularity. The fervor and commitment of social media participants overwhelmingly indicate that it is the most accurate and rational platform of information available on this planet. There is also an abundance of videos on social media, which depict the feline species in a variety of antics. I have found these cat videos to be a most uplifting diversion during my non-working hours.

While the coffee shop experiment appears dead, I would be amiss to exclude mention of farming, distribution, grocery, and medical/ emergency service industries in Gamma's global economy. Earth's residents regard these trades as "essential" and hail their workers as "heroes." Joshua gave minimal regard to these industries in his report, instead focusing attention on entertainment and financial investment circles of power. It is apparent that Joshua has been wooed by the sophisticated reputation of those industries on this satellite, as many of the younger of our species are. In time, Joshua will realize what you and I know: that the middle and low-level earners in a society are the heart of it. Without them, a society cannot sustain itself. Although Joshua's shortsightedness on this subject is remarkable, I cannot deny that we may have set him up for failure. He is inexperienced and naive and easily swayed by stereotypes he has heard about this species.

This brings me to a commentary on Gamma's communities in general, where my findings again contradict what young Joshua reported in his assessment. The "frenzied" lifestyle depicted in Joshua's summary is an exaggeration, if I am to be perfectly blunt. His tales of families going in different directions from morning until dark are a fabrication of the truth. Families do not scurry from work to school to fast food to evening activities on a daily basis. On the contrary, families spend many of their daytime hours together, pursuing productivity and learning via electronic aids and devices. Parents, in large part, work from home using computers and phones, and their work hours are flexible, beginning in the early morning for some and extending into evening hours for others. Families frequently take walks together in the evening and talk about the day's activities. There seems to be a much stronger and healthier family dynamic than Joshua suggested. This presents a complication to our plan of attack, as you can imagine. Much of our strategy depends on the diversion of residents' attention from the family unit to self-gratification, which is not as widespread and established as we originally thought.

Additionally, the education of young Gammaphites is not nearly as dysfunctional as Joshua indicated. While I feel face-to-face instruction would be more beneficial, the intensity and dedication of teachers to their students in virtual learning environments is unlike any I have witnessed in neighboring solar systems. The teachers provide both large group-learning opportunities and differentiated instruction to individuals, all accomplished digitally. Not only that, but the teachers give messages of love and support to their pupils, not wanting any one of them to feel ignored or discounted. Many schools feed their students, sending buses to their homes. It is as though students have both home families and school families who love and care for them. I do not understand how this is accomplished, as the funding allocations for schools do not indicate them as being a top priority. More research is indicated toward understanding the thoughts and behaviors of these "educators," as they are called here, who are managing much with little.

I must reveal, Orion, that Joshua's biggest miscalculation was in reporting on the foundations of human interaction. Humans do not enjoy the company of other humans outside their households, as Joshua described. I do not observe individuals gathering either for entertainment or for celebration in groups together. In fact, they avoid each other entirely, keeping their distance from each other in public places as much as possible. Our hypothesis that these creatures place great emphasis on social interactions, though supported by many of our peers and leading system minds, is certainly doubtful. Based on my current observations, I plan to initiate a revised archetype of the human species for our reference, which will prove to be the most modern and accurate account we have known.

One area in particular warrants additional investigation before we formulate an updated, accurate model of humans. I am not able to find any documentation on the prevalence of mask-wearers and non-mask-wearers in our literature. Joshua also did not mention this issue in any of his reports, to my consternation. There are clearly two factions of social infrastructure: people who wear masks outside of their homes and people who do not wear masks. These mutually exclusive groups tolerate each other in public. However, in private, they are exceedingly critical of each other. On social media, many of them take part in publicly shaming those in the opposite group, whether for mask-wearing or for not wearing masks. This is truly an intriguing topic, which we will explore more deeply in subsequent visits.

The most fascinating part of my account is still to be told, Orion. In the many years of surveillance in this solar system and many others, I never have observed a phenomenon more strange and unexpected. The humans have discovered a resource in a material previously thought to be very commonplace on this planet. The product, "toilet paper," is an item we had dismissed as being related to cleaning after defecation. There is, however, undoubtedly another use for the commodity. The humans buy this item at a frequency and volume that proves there must be more to toilet paper than pudendal freshness. Whether this resource satisfies a deeper medicinal purpose is unclear; perhaps it contains healing principles we have overlooked. It may be a more profound discovery, Orion. What if this paper contains an element previously undiscovered, which could aid in our efforts for dominion? I am pleased to tell you that after much searching, I have procured a sample of toilet paper by outwitting a local grocer, arriving early during senior shopping hours, and slipping past slower elderly mortals. The specimen is the very best quality: triple-ply double-rolls, equivalent to twenty-four regular rolls. I will forward this sample to our laboratories, where our scientists will examine it meticulously. I am sure you share in my excitement and expectancy to learn the results of these tests.

In summary, sir, I recommend that we suspend acquisition of the Gamma planet until we have more data. My findings are in such stark contrast to Joshua's report that I fear our current intelligence is proven inaccurate and creates potential for the failure of our mission. I recommend that we redirect the fourth and fifth aerial battalions, now headed at rapid speed toward Earth, to a new target in the Local Void. The new target should be well outside the Milky Way galaxy, where no toilet paper will be harmed. It is, after all, a priceless resource in this solar system, one which I am proud to play a part in discovering. I will report to your station at Virgo in short time. I urge you to consider a merciful repercussion for Joshua, as he is an inexperienced and unseasoned cadet who requires additional training. I am willing to take him under my tutelage, but in the meantime, I suggest he be assigned to mapping duties in one of the outer voids. This "terra incognito" is just the sort of challenge that will develop thoughtfulness and attention to detail in a young scout.

I remain your humble servant in pursuit of gaining supremacy of our super-cluster. Upon transmission of this message, I will begin the voyage back to Virgo. I regret that our ascendancy to power over Earth and the Milky Way is delayed. However, I think you will agree that postponement of our plan is the only prudent option. Along with the toilet paper, I bring with me an unexpected gift from one large government entity, called a stimulus check. Its origin and purpose are unclear, but many residents of the world received one, and I am happy to be included in that lot. Until I see you, Orion, I wish favor upon you and thank you for your unwavering trust in me.

Regards,
Moses
Second Lieutenant, Gamma Division
Virgo Cosmic Force

JEDWIN SMITH

Our Lives on Hold

FOLKS ARE CALLING IT A LOCKDOWN. AND RIGHTLY SO.
Reminds me of one of those old James Cagney and George
Raft prison movies in the 1930s. Cell doors locked tight. Murderous
felons reclining on bunks, reminiscing about evil deeds in their bad
ol' glory days. Awaiting the dreaded walk along the "Green Mile,"
where they will sit in a wooden chair attached to electrical wires.

Such is this COVID-19 bondage we've been dealt. To borrow
a line from one of my favorite Kris Kristofferson songs—"The
Pilgrim: Chapter 33"—I've come to view this China-spawned pandemic as "a blessing and a curse."

The curse is not being able to say goodbye. The blessing is indulg-
ing my passion for reading and writing a new book.

First the curse.

A number of friends and loved ones have been carried away in
death during this time. Most notably is my younger brother Joe.
A highly decorated U.S. Army Sergeant-Major, Joe retired after a
four-year hitch in the Marine Corps and almost three decades of
service after that. Pride of the Smith clan, Joe discovered at 68 that
he had stage four cancer of the larynx. Numerous radiation and
chemo treatments did not help. So, Joe gave the okay to an El Paso
surgeon to test his luck at experimental surgery, which had less than
a twenty-percent chance of success.

The procedure entailed removing his larynx and fashioning a new
one constructed from a section of his intestines, one-third of which

were also removed. The surgery was not successful, and, once again sacrificing himself on behalf of others, Joe bravely faced death and slipped into a coma from which he never regained consciousness.

Because of the stinkin' social-distancing scare, my brother died with only his wife holding his hands. All the rest of his vast extended family—including his five children, a passel of grandkids, nieces and nephews, and myself—were quarantined hundreds of miles away. Which pisses me off to no end. Especially since all this occurred in the shadow of Memorial Day.

Compounding this tragedy, my brother was to have had his remains interred at Virginia's Arlington National Cemetery on July 4, with family and friends in attendance. Due to the social-distancing panic, however, the ceremony has been postponed to Independence Day 2021.

So we wait.

Back in the early 1980s, Joe and I were in Beirut, Lebanon, working opposite ends of the religious bloodbath. He, a forward artillery observer on loan from the U.S. Army to the Foreign Legion, pinpointing enemy targets to be pulverized by French heavy guns. Me reporting on the carnage. We never were able to hook up in Beirut. Years later, Joe said he figured it must have been me his cohorts among the *Légion étrangère* were talking about when describing "the crazy, thrill-seeking American journalist disregarding his own safety."

Joe had a great sense of humor as well as a quirky philosophical outlook on life. Liked to say that while the Marine Corps had taught him how to throw the ball, it was the Army that had taught him how to control it. He also liked to kid me about my penchant for charging headfirst into prickly situations. Joe always viewed battlefield dilemmas with deep thought, then called in artillery support.

"Which," he often scolded me, borrowing from the wisdom of Yoda, his favorite Star Wars character, "most certainly prolongs one's life-span."

Hell, Joe had survived a multitude of combat tours on various foreign shores, always able to survive villainous folks trying to prematurely end his life—angry Panamanians to Lebanese Shiites, Syrians, and Palestinians; Yugoslavians of varying religious sects; Iraqis; and Iranians. My God, surviving all that danger only to die in a hospital bed in the far-western corner of Texas. As all the media pundits quip, "Such is the new norm."

Which sucks.

If I had my way, all those Chi-Coms—who, apparently, allowed the disease to slip through their fingers, accidently or not—would already have been strung up by their *cojones*.

To write this, I'm at my computer, putting aside the book I've been working on for the past two months wherein I reminisce about working as a newspaper reporter who is laboring to maintain sobriety. Taking time to count the roses, it's like discovering the Fountain of Youth. Once again I'm back in my glory days, doing what old folks are so fond of doing. Recollecting those good ol' days has done wonders for my mental well-being.

Family is a blessing. Which my wife and I keep telling ourselves over and over as we ride herd on four teenage grandsons, plus our youngest daughter, a single mom. Which means there's a lot of smiling going on to keep up joyous appearances for everyone's sake. Didn't help none that all the schools were shuttered, which equates to 24/7 wall-to-wall rambunctious adolescents.

To blot out all the noise in our three-ring circus, I've been binge-reading Craig Johnson, who wrote the Longmire series about a Wyoming sheriff. You might be familiar with the character from Netflix. This in addition to watching all the cowboy movies of yesterday.

Yippe-yi-yo, let me count the memories. There's Randolph Scott and Johnny Mack Brown, Lash Larue and Tex Ritter, Wild Bill Elliott and Crash Corrigan, Hopalong Cassidy and Joel McCrea, Gene Autry and Roy Rogers, Bob Steele, and the Cisco Kid. Not to forget John Wayne, James Stewart, and Gary Cooper.

My heroes have always been cowboys.

Thank God for Ted Turner's classic movie channel, plus the INSP (Heroes Live Here) channel, both of which take me down memory lane, visiting those old Western TV shows of my youth— *Gunsmoke, Wanted: Dead or Alive, The Rebel,* and *Have Gun – Will Travel,* just to name a few. And believe me, memory lane ain't all that bad, considering the perilous times we're going through right now.

Funny thing happened the other day. I was watching a young Steve McQueen (as bounty hunter Josh Randall) in a black-and-white televised pursuit of some villainous outlaws when Connor, one of our grandkids, joined me on the couch. Must have been at least five minutes of silence before he asked, "Who's that cowboy, Pops?"

"Why, you like this show?" was my response.

"Oh, it's okay… I guess. Why no color?"

Thought he was joking, so I said, "Because it was filmed back in the days before desegregation."

He merely nodded, his lack of American history evident. "That cowboy seems pretty cool, though."

Told him that cool cowboy was Steve McQueen, one of my favorite actors—rattlin' off some of his greatest hits: *The Great Escape, Papillon, The Magnificent Seven, Sand Pebbles, Nevada Smith, The Cincinnati Kid,* and *Bullitt.*

The kid's response? Just a simple "Huh." And then he retired to the grandkids' video-game room, which is really my library… well, it used to be my library, that is, until that fateful knock on our front door three years ago where, upon answering, one of our daughters and her three sons stood with smiles and duffel bags full of clothes and those fateful words: "Hey, Pops, could we please crash in your family room for a couple of nights?"

Wasn't long after that Skyler, another teenage video-gaming grandson from a different daughter's busted marriage, joined the family scrum, completing the circle that refuses to be unbroken. Guess you might say that's another of life's "new norms."

Ah, but who am I to complain?

If nothing else, the COVID-19 suppression has brought the family even closer together. Hell, I'm even starting to get better at placing correct names to the many faces, much to my wife's delight. June's response to whenever the kids push me to the edge of the abyss?

"You always wanted sons, right? Now we've got 'em."

Indeed… plus the accompanying grocery bill. They eat like a ravenous pack of wild dogs and suck down two gallons of milk a day. Yikes!

As for my library, I do venture—or should I say, trespass?—into the absconded sanctuary from time to time and remind the kids they have my permission to read any of the military historical volumes in the floor-to-ceiling bookshelves taking up two of the room's walls.

They reward me with silent, quizzical stares before mindlessly returning to blasting away at enemy aliens on their PlayStations.

And thus our lives are on hold in what some say is the new norm. But every black cloud has a silver lining. It's our job to focus on that lining so that, when we come through this—and we will—we'll be ready to hit the ground running.

Because that's what Americans do.

MARIN HENRY

Group Therapy

Dr. Aarons sat in a brown leather chair, writing notes on a clipboard. He rested his ankle on his knee and, every so often, stroked his salt-and-pepper beard. The sound of rhythmic ticking from a clock filled the room. It was a sad little room that looked more like a place where interrogations were held than an office. Nonetheless, Dr. Aarons's attempts to decorate the space were apparent. There was artwork hanging on all four of the walls. They were black-and-white photographs of flowers enclosed in solid black picture frames. Perhaps having pictures of flowers in color would have been too frilly for Dr. Aarons's tastes, so gray was used instead. There were a few potted plants that gave the drab office some much-needed life, as well. The pops of shades of green really made a difference in the room. Many of the plants were fake, but still their presence was appreciated.

Nailed above Dr. Aarons's desk was his doctorate degree from Emory University. It was there to assure patients he wasn't a quack; not that anyone would think so. Aarons was highly recommended and revered for his excellent work.

On his organized desk were photos of his wife and children. His wife was an attractive brunette with green eyes. She looked warm and fun-loving in the photo, like the kind of woman who could dance like a dork in a crowd full of people and not care one bit what they thought. The children were two boys, maybe eight and ten years old. They had their mother's green eyes, but the curly hair and caramel-toned skin came from Dr. Aarons. They looked like a picture-perfect family, so happy and filled with love. Aarons kept that photo there on his desk to give himself a smile whenever he needed it, and in his line of work, it was needed often.

He continued writing. The faint sound of scribbling could be heard if you listened carefully enough. A small wrinkle from deep concentration separated his brows. He was a good-looking man. The kind of man who could be described as debonair. His looks paired with his intelligence. His charm would have been more than enough reason for him to be cocky, but he wasn't. He was sincere, humble, and kind. This was something that made him even more attractive.

Finally, after some time, his writing slowed to an end. He set the clipboard down on his lap and rested his interlaced fingers on top of it. He then softly cleared his throat and spoke.

"Thank you for waiting so patiently, and thank you for being here today. I'm excited about this. Aren't you?" He waited for a response, but there was none. A few seconds of awkward silence passed, and then he continued. "Let's get started, then, shall we? Why don't you tell me about yourself."

He smiled, expecting a response. A few more moments passed, but still there was only silence.

"Okay, how about I start?" suggested Aarons in an attempt to salvage the uncomfortable situation. "My name is Dr. Eli Aarons. I'm a licensed psychologist. I live in Decatur, Georgia, with my wife and children. When I'm not working, I enjoy cooking or watching soccer with my two boys."

He beamed. He couldn't conceal the pride he felt in his sons, even if he tried. He was a true family man. He raised one thick eyebrow as though to say *Now it's your turn to speak.* Finally, after what seemed like an eternity, a young woman looked up from staring at the floor and introduced herself.

"I'm Mara," she said, just above a whisper.

Aarons tried to reassure her with a smile and responded gently, "Hi, Mara. It's nice to meet you. Where, may I ask, are you from?"

She rolled her eyes and grinned. "Respectfully, Doctor," she began, "I know what you're trying to do."

Aarons adjusted in his seat. "Oh? And what might that be?" he asked, being especially careful not to convey a snarky tone.

"You think if you pretend to want to get to know me, then I'll let my guard down and spill my guts about myself." Mara had a right to be suspicious. If history had taught her anything, it was that people couldn't be trusted. As far as she was concerned, there was nothing for her to say to this stranger. Still, Aarons couldn't help but laugh.

"Well, nothing gets past you," he said with a sly grin. Mara grinned right back at him.

"That's right," she replied, folding her arms and leaning back in her chair, quite pleased with herself for not having fallen for any of his mind games. "I don't trust anybody or anything."

Aarons exhaled. "Well, we have an entire hour together," he said, glancing up at the wall clock. "There's no pressure, and I don't have any expectations. Let's just get to know each other. I already told you where I'm from—what's the harm in you returning the favor?"

Mara stared at Aarons for a long moment. Her eyes narrowed. She was sizing him up, trying to figure him out. But she couldn't tell if he was sincere or not. Nonetheless, he was right. No harm in a little small talk. She let out a breath and looked back down at the floor.

"I grew up in Athens," she said with a grudge in her voice.

Dr. Aarons's expression brightened. "Oh, so you've lived abroad in Greece?"

He chuckled, satisfied with himself for the corny joke, but Mara wasn't as amused. She rolled her eyes again and pursed her lips, but she still couldn't entirely manage to hide a half-smile.

Aarons continued. "I have a few friends who went to UGA. You think you might know them?"

Mara shook her head. "I doubt it. Attending a big university wasn't really my thing."

Aarons nodded. "I can understand that. Well, what about hobbies or interests that you have?"

She responded with a raised eyebrow.

"I told you mine, remember?" he said, knowing exactly what her look meant.

She shrugged. "I enjoy reading." Her eyes met Aarons's for just a second.

"Oh, really? What are you reading currently?" he asked with genuine interest. Against her better judgement, she could feel herself becoming a little more relaxed.

"*Alice's Adventures in Wonderland,*" she replied. "It's one of my favorites. I reread it all the time."

Aarons smiled. "That's a great book. I read it to my boys a while back, and they loved it. Lewis Carroll definitely had a big imagination."

Mara smiled in agreement. She was starting to warm up to him despite her efforts not to. He had such an endearing presence, and it was nearly impossible to resist his charm. But he couldn't hide a puzzled look.

"Is there any particular reason why you chose that book?"

Mara's smile faded. She thought for a second, then shrugged. "I like fiction, especially fantasy. It's always been my favorite genre."

Aarons nodded as though he understood, but his puzzled look remained. "When did you start becoming interested in those types of books?" he asked.

Mara thought back as far as she could before responding, "I guess when I was about seven."

Aarons nodded again. He settled more into his seat and stroked his beard, then probed a bit further. "What are some memories that you have from that time? What was life like for you back then?"

Mara wrung her hands, unable to hide her agitation. A deep wrinkle appeared between her brows. She was uncomfortable, and Aarons knew it.

"It's okay," he reassured her. "Just start from the beginning. Remember, there's no judgment here."

Mara's eyes glossed over, and she stared past Dr. Aarons. She was physically there, but mentally, she was as distant as one could be. Her face was emotionless. "We... We lived in an old house." Uncertainty crept into her response.

"Go on," Aarons encouraged her.

"Mama worked a lot, and Daddy, well, he just drank. I remember they fought constantly. But when Mama wasn't there to take the beatings, then Daddy would turn his attention to me." She was still wringing her hands, only now more vigorously.

"How did that make you feel?"

Mara scoffed. "Is that seriously a question? I was a child and was terrified, so obviously not great."

"Sorry. Dumb question," he admitted. "What would you do when your father behaved that way?"

Mara's gaze darted away to hide the tears that were beginning to form. Her once-vacant expression was now replaced with pain. "I would go to my room, hide under the bed, and cry," she replied with a slight quiver in her voice. "Then, after a while had passed, I'd pick up a book and read."

Aarons pulled two Kleenex tissues from a box on the wooden table next to him. He leaned forward and extended them to Mara. But before she took them, there was an abrupt interruption.

"Hi!" a sweet, shy little voice greeted him, catching him off-guard. Hearing the voice, his whole demeanor changed. His once-serious expression became more lighthearted.

"Well, hello, and who might you be?"

Two big doe-eyes met his own. "My name is Brianne."

A smile spread across Dr. Aarons's face. "Well, that's a pretty name. How old are you, Brianne?"

She held up her hand, showing five fingers. "I'm five years old," she said proudly, batting the lashes of her beautiful, wide eyes.

"Well, you're practically a lady," said Aarons, pleasing Brianne. "Is there something else you want to say to me?"

Brianne nodded enthusiastically. Dr. Aarons leaned forward.

"Well, let's hear it, sweetie, and thank you for waiting so patiently."

Brianne smiled from ear to ear. "Well," she began, "my favorite food in the whole world is pizza!"

Aarons chuckled. This bit of information couldn't have been more off-topic or unimportant, but he indulged her.

"Really?" Aarons asked. "That's one of my favorites, too. Please, go on."

He hung on her every word, and she loved every minute of his attention.

"My most favorite color is yellow, like the sun."

She talked on and on, sharing anything she thought Aarons might like to hear. She went down an endless list of all her favorite things—her favorite animal, favorite song, favorite ice cream flavor, and so on. Then, once she decided she was done with her list of favorites, she moved on to knock-knock jokes, ones that were so cheesy that you laughed simply because they were so bad, not because of a witty punchline. Brianne had such a spunky, happy-go-lucky personality. Aarons quite enjoyed his conversation with her, perhaps because it was a nice change of pace from the troubled adults he normally dealt with.

"You sound like a pretty awesome kid, Brianne," Aarons said, raising his hand to give her a high-five. "You must have more friends than you can count."

Brianne slapped his hand, then glanced at the ceiling, as though she were counting her friends.

"Um, I guess, but actually, my best friend is Coco!" Brianne's smile widened.

"Tell me about her."

"Well," Brianne began, "we always have fun together. We go on all sorts of adventures. We go to the moon and eat cheese, fight pirates on the ocean, and even wrestle lions."

"Sounds like you two have a very vivid imagination," Aarons said with a chuckle.

Brianne's head bobbed energetically. She was proud to have a big imagination. It was something she thought made her special.

"Well, someday, I hope to meet Coco," Aarons said. "She seems almost as awesome as you." Brianne cocked her head to the side and gave Aarons a confused look.

"You can't see Coco," she said nonchalantly. "Only I can. Coco is make-believe."

Aarons leaned back in his chair and rubbed his chin. A child having an imaginary friend wasn't anything abnormal, but he was curious. "Coco is imaginary?"

"Yeah, I thought her up all by myself!" Brianne boasted.

"Do you ever play with your real friends, too? Maybe there's a classmate that you get along really well with."

Brianne shook her head. "No, she's my only friend. The kids at school are mean, but Coco is always nice."

Aarons opened his mouth to respond, but Brianne jumped in before he could speak.

"You know what's the best thing about Coco?" she asked. "She never has to leave." There was a slight smile on her face, but a deep sadness in her voice. Aarons had started to ask a few more questions when yet another interruption intruded.

"Ahem. How much longer am I going to have to sit around and wait for you?"

Dr. Aarons sat up in his seat, the cool leather peeling off his back.

"Er, yes. Uh, hello," Aarons said clumsily. A laugh filled the room.

"How very articulate of you, Doctor." The sarcastic remark would have been fine if said playfully, but it definitely wasn't. This visitor was obviously annoyed. Aarons attempted a friendly introduction.

"Apologies. It's nice to meet you, mister, uh—"

"Just call me Nick." His tone was bone-dry.

Aarons reached out his hand and waited a moment for Nick to do the same. When it became clear the intruder wasn't going to respond, Aarons withdrew his hand to his lap, abandoning the idea of a polite greeting. Dr. Aarons wasn't quite sure why, but it was clear Nick was harboring some animosity against him. He bounced his knee, uncertain how to continue. Nick smirked, taking note of Aarons's body language.

"Do I make you nervous, Doctor?" The question made Aarons stop the nervous tic immediately. He let out a breath and forced a smile. He steadied himself before proceeding.

"So tell me about yourself."

Nick crossed his arms. "Actually, Doc, I'd rather tell *you* about yourself."

Aarons adjusted in his seat.

"You're nothing but a joke," Nick said. "Absolutely pathetic. You think you're so big with your fancy office and degree, but you're not. Everyone worships the ground you walk on, but I know the truth, and deep down, so do you: you're nothing."

Aarons kept his composure but still was startled by Nick's comments. There was such anger and power behind them. Aarons made sure to choose his next words carefully so as not to upset Nick further.

"Nick, I don't know if I've done something to upset you, but if so, allow me to apologi—"

Nick put his hand up. "Save it," he said, cutting Aarons off. "You're not going to charm your way out of this one."

They both sat for a few moments in silence. Aarons was running out of ideas. He wanted to break through to Nick, but there was a wall there that he just couldn't get past. He studied Nick. There was anger in his eyes, but if Aarons's job had taught him anything, it was that anger was a fear-based emotion. Beneath Nick's hot-headed demeanor was nothing but pain and insecurity. If Aarons could just tap into that, then perhaps they could make some progress.

"What?!" Nick blurted out, annoyed and uncomfortable that Aarons was observing him.

"Apologies, Nick," Aarons said sincerely. "You have so much pent up inside of you. I'd like to help you with that, if you'll allow me."

Nick scoffed. "I don't need or want your help."

At this point, he wasn't even looking Dr. Aarons in the eye anymore. It was as though he were disgusted by the very sight of him. Aarons took no offense. Such was part of the job. He simply wanted to help.

"I know it can be difficult to open up about these things, but there's no need to be scared."

Nick shot Aarons a nasty look. "What the hell are you talking about?" he asked, offended by the idea. "I'm not afraid of anything."

Aarons smiled. "There's no need to get upset. Everyone is afraid of something. Perhaps you are afraid of appearing weak if you admit your pain."

This upset Nick even more. "Careful, Doc!" Nick warned through clenched teeth, his fists tight.

Dr. Aarons could see Nick was becoming more unnerved, but he pushed further. This may not have been the most orthodox form of counseling, but it seemed to be working. Although Aarons felt bad provoking such strong emotions in Nick, in his opinion, it was much better than keeping them bottled up and unresolved.

"Nick, please. There's no need to put on a front. Who do you have to be so brave for? Who are you trying to impress here? Who has hurt you?"

Nick jumped up from his chair with such force that the chair shot behind him.

"Shut up!" Nick barked. He might as well have had smoke coming out of his ears. He stared at Aarons with rage in his eyes. Aarons stood up to be eye-level with him.

"If you don't let this out, then it will control you forever!" Aarons said. "You'll prove you're a coward if you don't confront these emotions."

With that, Nick lunged, grabbing Dr. Aarons by the collar. He yanked him close. Aarons tried to pull free but was unsuccessful. Aarons could see Nick was past the point of reason, in a blind fury. He could smell the stench of Nick's breath and could feel the droplets that hit his face with every word Nick spoke.

"Don't you ever call me that!" Nick shouted, violently shaking Aarons. "I'm not a coward! I'm not afraid of you, Dad!"

Aarons blinked. Confusion emerged on his face, and he focused on Nick. "Dad?" he repeated softly.

Nick loosened his grip on Aarons's collar. He was huffing, and tears streaked down his cheeks. He broke his glare and looked beyond Aarons. The anger melted from his face and was replaced with surprise. He was shocked by the way he had exploded and by what he had said.

"Is that what this is all about? Is he the one who hurt you?" Aarons asked, never breaking his stare.

Nick turned back to Aarons. He tightened his grasp on the doctor's collar again. "Stay the hell away from me," he growled. He shoved Aarons and started to walk off, done with the entire situation.

"Wait!" Aarons started, reaching out to touch his arm. "Let's finish this. Let's talk calmly and rat—"

Nick grabbed the hand on his forearm and twisted. "I said no!"

"Please, stop!" Aarons said, stifling a scream.

Nick shoved Aarons, and the doctor stumbled back, falling on top of the wooden table that held the tissues, shattering it. Aarons lay on the floor, squeezing his eyes shut and rubbing his throbbing wrist.

"Stop this, Nick!" Aarons pleaded from the cold, hard floor.

Another interruption, this time the sound of a woman's voice. Everything seemed to come to a halt.

"Eli? Is that you?"

Aarons opened one eye, and he saw he was no longer in his office. He opened his second eye and frantically looked around. He was alone in a dim room with a concrete floor. There were boxes, furniture, knick-knacks, and cobwebs all over. His breath quickened and he began to sweat.

"Wha—What's going on? Where am I?!" He squeezed his eyes shut again, convincing himself that this must be some sort of dream, or rather a nightmare, and if he opened his eyes again, it would all go away. But fear's grip on him was too strong. He couldn't force himself to open his eyes. The woman's voice called out again, only this time much closer and clearer.

"Eli? What are you doing out of bed? And what did you do to the basement?"

"Leave me alone. Leave me alone!" he shouted back in the direction of the voice.

He heard footsteps approaching and the sound of a light switching on. The darkness behind his eyelids became a little brighter. Unexpectedly, he felt two soft hands hold the sides of his face.

"Eli, open your eyes, please." The voice was right in front of him, and he could smell perfume. Aarons blinked to see an attractive brunette with green eyes kneeling in front of him.

"It's okay, my love," she said in a soothing tone. "You're home and you're safe."

Aarons collapsed in his wife's arms and wept. She stroked his head gently and made soft shushing sounds.

"I just want them to go away," cried Aarons. "I can't get these delusions out of my head."

Aarons's wife wiped away a tear with her thumb.

"We're going to get you some help. We're going to fix this together."

She stood up and extended her hand to help her husband up from the floor. He stood, and she wrapped her arm around him while he laid his head on her shoulder. They walked side by side up the creaky basement stairs, leaving the darkness behind.

TERRA ELAN MCVOY

Covid-19 2020: A Narrow Slice of What It Is Like

Day One: Immediate Thoughts

First: wash all the surfaces.
This means doorknobs,
light switches,
and every bathroom faucet.
Flush handle and the back of the toilet.
The towel rack.
The table.
The cabinet handles.
The sink.
Wash your hands and wash them all again.
Even the inside of the car is not safe.
Neither are the grocery bags.
Go back, wash your hands.
When was the last time this towel was in the laundry?
Which doorknob did you forget?

Next

Communicate with all the people.
Family and the best of friends, first.
You need to know how they are doing.
You need them to know how you are doing.
You all need to know how you are doing with how you are doing.

Soon, *everyone* will need to know how you are doing. And you will
need to know how they are doing. You will all need to know what
you are doing instead of doing the things you normally would be
doing, and how you are doing with that.

How are they doing?
How are you doing?
Tell them.
Ask them.
And then go back and check again.

And Then

Narrate in other ways.
Emails,
phone calls,
social posts,
a new app called Marco Polo
(Why haven't you been using it all your life?),
video calls, more phone calls, even actual mail.
Zoom becomes its own essential worker.
You are starting to take specific notes.

At the same time: check the news.
Check the feed.
Then check back to the news and the feed and then back again.

Share all you find—even with people you haven't spoken to in years—
and go back to see what else has been found.

Communicate and narrate.

Now go wash your hands and then your phone.
Somehow it becomes a pantoum.

Masks

Remember February?
When you rolled your eyes
at that young couple wearing them in the airport?
Thinking
they were just being overdramatic? Making
an attention-grabbing statement?

Yeah. That was cute of you.

Day Twenty-One or -Two: Work

6.6 million unemployed—in weeks it will become 15, then 21, then more.
But not you. Not yet.
Instead work has ramped up
and you have risen to it.
Of course you will make and promote those webinars.
Update the needless spreadsheet.
Extend your hours.
Extend your days.
And then extend them again.
There will be no gardening for you.
No afternoons of crafting, or piecing vintage puzzles.
You will not bake bread or binge-watch or clean out that drawer.

Instead you will be grateful, and guilty
because at least you don't have children
—and it is 6.6 million of them and not you.

Grocery Shopping

The empty shelves are not a rumor.
Toilet paper, of course, and rice, cleaning products—all wiped out.
Still you can get
all the gluten free pasta
and birdseed
you can carry.

Remind yourself how fortunate you are.
And then go wash your hands.
Remember the inside of the car is unsafe.
Not to mention this box of Wheat Thins.

Day Thirty

It is time to start drinking in earnest.
Narrate this. Be honest. Be kind to yourself.
This is a pandemic the world has not quite seen before.
People are dying.
6.6 million unemployed (which soon will be 15, then 21, then more,
but not you).
Hospitals all over the country don't have enough equipment.
More cases sweep the land.
Check the news.
Check the feed.
Work some more.
Buy two bottles of wine instead of one.
Line the bottles along your sink.

Be grateful.
Wash your hands.
Wash your hands.

An Alternative To Baking Bread

Exercise: walks, rowing, yoga—it is Important to stay active.
And communicate how active you are.
Try new workouts,
new routes,
new routines.
Wipe down the weights, then lift them again.
Go for another walk.
Find yourself surrounded by sudden cyclists, everywhere.
Come home, wash your hands,
and then go narrate.

Six Weeks: Comparatively Speaking

There are things you miss so much:
restaurants,
a pedicure,
hot dogs at a soccer match,
making plans for—anything,
hugging a friend.

Meanwhile, nurses don't have enough equipment.
Thousands of cases sweep the land.
Whole towns will vanish.
Entire industries will not survive.

Outside the hospitals,
refrigerator trucks full of corpses hum.

Day Forty Five

Longer than Noah was in his Ark.
Longer than Jesus in the deserts.

Somewhere someone else is documenting this better.

Coda

Wash your hands check your feed drink some more be forgiving be grateful wash your hands do yoga go for a walk work late check the feed how are your friends it is all over drink some more be grateful do some work you are all dead check your feed why aren't you writing?

On Trying to Write About Day Sixty, When it Has Been 120

In spite of your notes, there is still so much you did not narrate.
And so much on day sixty you did not yet know.
You did not know, for example,
that Memorial Day weekend things would try to reopen
and the cases would spike.
You didn't know how good it would feel,
watching the trees green through their spring.
Or—even now—
when you will see your family in person.
Let alone get on a plane.

You did not know then
that the bar you liked so much
would soon go out of business,
and you won't remember
the last time you were there.

There's so much you didn't know yet.
Like the murders,
and the protests.
The ensuing riots.

Even today, you don't know what will happen.
You don't know what you will be narrating
next month on your birthday,
let alone next week,
or when the trees change color into Fall.
You don't know about the economy.
You don't know about the future.
You don't know if you will keep your job, keep your friends, keep
your sanity,
keep your hope.

Be grateful.
Check the feed.
Wear your mask.
Wash your hands.

Three million cases and counting.
There is so much you did not narrate.
And yours is only a very narrow slice of what it is like.

NEDRA PEZOLD ROBERTS

COVID Confinement, with a Nod to Christopher Durang

I'M A PLAYWRIGHT. THAT MEANS I SPEND A LOT OF TIME ALONE in my head. Sure, my characters visit me there from time to time, but, on the whole, I swim in a stream of silence.

Now, you would think that a steady diet of solitude would have prepared me for COVID Confinement.

You'd be wrong.

Sure, the media and online blogs are full of coping suggestions to get us through each meaningless day.

Exercise. Check.

Practice yoga breathing. Check.

Keep a diary.

A diary?

Are you *kidding* me???

In this pandemic, every day is Monday with an endless week stretching ahead.

I'm in isolation, stuck in season 42, episode 80 of *Survivor*. My daily routine is punctuated with large glasses of the furlough Merlot, which, as you can see, is helping me to fatten the curve. I wake up, eat, write, eat, shower, eat, then sleep so I can wake up and eat and write and eat…

Until the Earth dies!

I should mention that there are two exceptions to my routine. First, texting has become a fulltime job. I'm at the beck and call of everyone desperate to share instant inanities. Life is so very small these days.

Second, there's Zoom, where I now spend more time than I used to in actual human gatherings. This is the new way writers get their work heard: group readings that struggle to take the place of live theatre. We all sign on to the Zoom "meeting," and the computer's monitor fills up with tiny boxes that we sit in like the Brady Bunch, straining to catch every member's words that crackle in and out of a spotty microphone and intermittent speakers.

ONE OF MY friends advised me, "Go for a walk."

Yeah, right. My go-to outing is a quick jog to the Kroger on the corner.

Yesterday, I was minding my own business, shopping responsibly. I mean, I was wearing my mask and gloves, using my Lysol wipe for the shopping-cart handle, and consulting my list to keep myself from dawdling.

Get in, get out.

Stay safe.

And I was doing that, stashing a few essentials in my cart. I was following all the rules.

But not a lot of others got the memo. All around me were Covidiots who ignored the rules.

They weren't distancing or paying attention to the one-way-only aisles. They would abandon their carts in the middle of an aisle to read the label on a can. Touching, touching, touching everything. Or just standing there, staring at rows of empty shelves as though waiting for Kleenex and rolls of toilet paper to magically appear.

It was enough to make my head explode.

And then the stock boy in aisle five asked me, "You need anything?"

I was speechless.

That's the kind of question that invades your psyche and takes up residence in your pit of insecurity.

Do I need anything?

I thought, why yes. Yes. I need safety. Sanity. Sex!

Yeah, I know. I need sex.

Human touch, physical affection.

Look, I broke up with my boyfriend right before the world shut down, and now I live alone.

I don't even have a cat.

Or a house plant.

I am the fricking definition of *one*!

Usually, people look in the mirror to admire themselves. I do it to pretend there's another person keeping me company.

Anyway, in the middle of my silent freak-out, that stock boy scurried to the far end of the aisle and pretended to arrange rows of laundry soap.

So, I made my way over to the produce section—where I stopped to contemplate a perfectly round artichoke.

Now, I already had broccoli at home, so I really didn't need another vegetable. I took a deep yoga breath, priding myself on my restraint, and rolled my cart over to the tomatoes and squash. But that artichoke was whispering my name.

What could I do?

I sidled back over to the artichoke to contemplate its mysterious allure.

I was trying to decide if I really needed it or if it would simply be an impulse buy when another clerk approached me. Admittedly, I *may* have looked like a creepy artichoke stalker.

Judgment is everywhere in the produce section.

The clerk asked, "Can I help you?"

Sweet baby cheeses. Another one of *those* questions.

I looked into his eager, innocent eyes and considered how to answer. I mean, it was actually an existential question. So, like a Zen master, I softly chanted "Awakening Together" (in Japanese, of course) and waited for enlightenment.

He blinked, then held up both hands and slowly backed away.

I snatched up the artichoke, tossed it into my cart, and then casually approached the nearby grapes.

Those plump green bunches stared at me, daring me to sneak a test taste while wearing a mask. I furtively scouted the area and noticed a clerk eyeing me suspiciously from over by the Vidalia onions. The grapes sat there, smug, taunting me, as though they *knew* I'd back down.

Dammit.

Defeated, I rolled my cart to the checkout line. When had life become so *exhausting*?

I was stacking my meager purchases onto the conveyer belt when the checker cheerfully asked, "Did you find everything you were looking for?"

Oh. My. Lanta!

Did I find everything I was looking for?

No!

No I did not!

I slammed my carton of eggs on the conveyer belt and shouted as thick goo slowly leaked onto the counter. "I'm looking for world peace! A way to save the planet! But I can't even find the hand sanitizer!"

Customers, checkers, stock clerks—everyone froze. In the heavy silence, the loudspeaker blared, "Cleanup on checkout counter three!"

Then suddenly the world lurched back into motion.

The manager hustled over to me, snapping his fingers and mumbling something through his mask. I couldn't tell if he was muttering at me or someone else, but in a few moments, a stock boy came running with a fresh carton of eggs.

While the checkout counter was being scrubbed and my groceries were being bagged, an elderly woman steered her walker toward me. She was holding a small bottle of hand sanitizer.

"Take this one, dear," she said. "I was buying the last two, but we all need to share, don't we?"

As I left the store, a small shopping bag in each hand, I heard someone call a muffled goodbye.

I craned my neck, looking over my shoulder for—I'm not sure.
A lone shopper was waving at me, her squinty eyes smiling.
At least, I think it was a smile.
It's hard to tell when you're wearing a mask.

ANJALI ENJETI

When Senior Year Disappears

MY DREAMS LATELY HAVE BEEN VIVID. THEY RECALL THE final months of my senior year in high school—the pranks, the prom, the parties, the senior trip, and of course, the graduation. When I wake, I peruse old photos from that year. My friends and I are laughing, hugging, cheering. Our raised eyebrows, our winks, our peace signs, and our irreverent middle fingers give off a sense of daring and bravado, of silliness, of a heightened sense of confidence that shields a healthy dose of teen angst. Above all else, amid the fading colors and the warped photo paper, there is camaraderie and physical intimacy. Our arms are wrapped around one another so tightly it's as though we are helium-filled balloons. We're afraid that if we let go, we might float away.

My dreams parallel what my firstborn child should be experiencing right now. She is a high school senior completing her final months of her education online. Her senior class trips have been cancelled, as has her prom. Her graduation ceremony will take place online. Every senior will also have the opportunity to take photos in caps and gowns, one at a time while social distancing, on the same high school football field where they once filled the bleachers and cheered for their home team.

Unlike the end of my own senior year, where we disembarked, unfettered and free, the world has hit pause on the dawning of my daughter's well-earned adulthood. Her future is an infinite ellipse that extends far beyond three dots, into the unknown.

When she was born, her pediatrician in his starched doctor's coat suggested we minimize her contact in public for the first few months of her life to give her immune system a chance to blossom. Guests should wash their hands rigorously with soap and water before holding her and cough into bent elbows. I cleaned and disinfected every surface of our home to create a bubble of protection around my new baby. I bathed every inch of her body gently with a soft cloth, plied open the creases of tiny fists and infant flesh, and swaddled her tightly. During our hibernation, my chest was her source of food, my heartbeat her shelter.

Some eighteen years later, it feels as though we have returned to the beginning. For four months, now, we have mainly stayed at home. We have pushed contact with the world to the other side of an invisible membrane. My daughter should be on the verge of taking flight, but on the eve of her journey, we have clipped her wings and settled her more firmly into our family's nest. *Not yet, little bird. Not yet.*

She spends her days trying to recreate her life in a two-dimensional realm. She and her friends play *Catan* online and stream Netflix together. They keep in touch via Facetime, text, Instagram, and Snapchat. By now, many of these high school seniors have endured tragedy, abuse, bullying, illness, discrimination, and the very real fear of school shootings. Since kindergarten, their friendships and the communities they've built have been their anchors. And now they must keep them at a distance at the very same time a global pandemic collides head-on with one of life's major milestones.

Earlier this spring, she and her five best friends got dressed for a makeshift prom in their high school parking lot. Each one of them assumed a parking space, those white parallel lines harsh enforcers of social distancing. The air between them felt like a vast gulf, a vacuum that sucked away the years they'd spent joined at the hip like a row of paper dolls.

We parents donned facemasks and aimed smartphones. We arranged them in poses that made them seem as though they were closer together than they really were. *These photos are an illusion*, I wanted to shout out to them. *Your friendships are not.*

Don't ever forget it. They smiled and giggled, but their sadness was palpable. Their grief mirrored the gray skies above and the concrete below. Their senior years will not end with the confetti, toasts, and graduation caps tossed high into the air that they deserve. They will not experience the same sense of wonder and freedom we parents felt as we crossed the stage to receive our own diplomas. And try as we might in an empty parking lot, we will never be able to recreate the moments and the memories that our beloved seniors will miss.

We parents are grieving, too. Our job, after their births, was to transform them into decent, responsible, independent adults. It was easier said than done. Early on, we realized there was only so much we could control, and only so much we could protect our babies from. We learned that as parents, we are not so much steering the ship as sitting in the very back corner, trying to shout out directions or warnings above the waves crashing into the hull.

The pandemic has stamped a question mark across our roles as parents, too. We have spent years preparing ourselves for this moment, their inevitable departures, their surge into adulthood, and now we walk together in the midst of a sandstorm. We can't see what lies ahead.

PRESIDENT OBAMA, THE first president in the Class of 2020's memory, embodied the hope we had for them. Yet their four years of high school have coincided with the worst presidency in U.S. history. They were freshmen when President Trump was elected, and they are losing out on the remainder of their senior year because of his recklessness. These seniors now carry a heavy burden. They know full well that it's up to them to change the dire circumstances they find themselves in.

Perhaps our graduating seniors have found a way to forge different kinds of moments and memories. As they mask up for outdoor gatherings, they are learning how to rally around one another in creative ways during a catastrophe. They are mastering meaningful forms of communication and finding infinite ways to express their love for one another, despite the neighborhoods or miles between them. These resilient, big-hearted seniors are figuring out, together, how to survive this pandemic. And in doing so, they have embarked on a kind of communal bonding that goes far deeper than what I forged during my own senior year.

After an hour of prom photographs, our kids in their formalwear seemed spent. The petals of the girls' bouquets had begun to wilt. The boys grew restless in their stiff jackets. As they approached one another to say their goodbyes, their tall bodies, many exceeding the heights of their parents, formed a circle. It reminded me of the last time they had all been at my home in February, huddled together in my basement, talking excitedly with one another about their boundless futures when those futures had still felt set in stone.

February. It is a month that now feels many more moons ago.

Soon after it formed, one child then another broke the sacred ring of friendship and drifted back slowly to their parents. I tried to imagine a different kind of reunion for them, and a different ending, one full of hugs and high-fives and long, tight embraces. Someday, I hoped, these friends would find their way back to one another at a time that made more sense to us all.

My own senior approached our car and opened the door, her pale pink gown billowing in the breeze. We had purchased this dress some time before, when we could never have foreseen a prom in a parking lot. Though I suppose not much about parenting or new adulthood is ever foreseeable. We are all wading through deep waters, unable to know or trust what's hovering just below the surface.

"That was kind of sad," she said, sighing, as she watched her friends depart through the window. "But it's time for us to go home."

I drove out of the parking lot as the parents with their children disappeared into their own cars, and I watched them fade, smaller and smaller, until I could no longer see them from my rearview mirror.

GWYNDOLYN D. PARKER

Lady Liberty Resurrected

It was eight minutes and forty-six seconds
That set off the second midnight ride of Paul Revere.
The cries went out far and wide, and the world rose to hear
The clarion-call of the faithful and declared their allegiance, too;
The revolution that was needed to combat and erase
The impending desecration of the United States.
Worrying voices cluttered the airwaves and the streets
And continued, as on auto-repeat.
No bullets, tear gas, or pepper spray
Could deter the crowds on their way
To seek justice day after day
For the lives of too many that had been taken away.
It swept around the world; racism was on trial
That had been kept in place in a systematic style.
Generation after generation had been subjugated
By the things those with "white privilege" in the world could do.
White people woke up, and their children, too,
And said a world like this would no longer do.
For it was a world they had not bought into;
It was Independence Day, the Fourth of July,
But it was just another day for me
In a country where I have neither been independent nor free.
Oh, America, America, where no grace was left to see.
Everyone saw what we saw; there is no teeming shore.

My country 'tis of thee had died for lack of me.
From sea to shining sea, there is no mourning thee.
First went the safeguards over the rails
That kept our lives from being a living hell.
Heard were the outcries, to no avail.
No one was left in power to help.
The poor, the jobless, and the hungry wept.
"Oh, say, can you see the humanity in me?"
It was just as it was with the first midnight ride of Paul Revere
That signaled danger for all to hear.
But this time, those who rallied from their beds
Cared not if others barely lifted their head.
For we already knew democracy was dead.
The Statue of Liberty sank into the river of her tears.
She drowned because of all her fears
That the land she stood on was no more.
That where had welcomed huddled masses yearning to breathe free
Now belonged to those who stood in the background
And watched while Lady Liberty sank and drowned.
No lamp to lift beside the golden door
Whose light was put out to shine no more.
All aspirations gone, all empathy buried,
For greed and avarice, power had married.
It was in this backdrop we stood,
Poised and clear-eyed to take back what we could.
The powerless, the weak, the hungry, the meek,
We were all in this together, for justice we seek.
Oh, say, can you see by the dawn's early light:
A new country was rising out of the night.
We wrote a new story and sang a new song
That told of a new country about to be born
By the sweat of the brow of all who have mourned,
For the millions who had suffered, morning, noon, and night,
While the country's forgotten struggled to get things right.
A congressional hearing was held; the truth came out.

Nothing had been early enough to help with the fight.
Then we began a new day, equal in footing, equal in pay,
Equal in consequence, equal in how far we could soar,
Equal as people whoever we are.
A new foundation built up from the ground
By people with a heart would be sound,
Able to stand proud and strong
Against all that had gone very wrong.
America the beautiful is no more;
This new country will be so much more.
For we the people will build on truth
And hold ourselves accountable as real proof
To the things we must do.
Never asking what this country can do for us
But building a country that will do for all
As we do for it, gratefully standing tall.
We created new ways to heal the Earth
So that everyone had a place
To blend into one human race.
Then during it all, my country 'tis of thee
Did truly become the land of liberty,
The land for all who seek equality.
We learned from our past and celebrated our future.
Faced the horrors never with being repeated, but to grow from
And brought our children into a world that valued everyone.
Looking into their eyes and the future we have perceived,
We hope that they will never say, "I can't breathe!"

SONIAH KAMAL

My Mother Calls Me from Pakistan

My mother calls me from Pakistan. "Soniah, *meri jaan*," she says, "stock up on disposable gloves, the surgical kind, and face masks."

Could it be a case of exaggeration?

No. Yes.

Mothers do exaggerate for reasons galore.

My mother is an anesthesiologist, and doctors always see the worst because they know the worst. These disposable gloves my mother recommends are the kind that doctors wear during surgery: rubbery from the outside, powdery from the inside. They are not those transparent types that come with hair-coloring kits so that you don't stain your skin but rip so easily. Growing up, there was always a box of surgical gloves at home. It was in the cabinet with the first-aid kit: Band-Aids, aspirin, a bottle of gentian violet, cotton balls, and white surgical gloves. The box with gloves resembled a particularly pedestrian box of tissues: rectangle with a lone stripe across the top. In my house, they were used for all purposes. My mother wore them to peel garlic so her hands would not stink.

*

MY MOTHER CALLS me from Pakistan. "Soniah, *meri jaan*, stock up on disposable gloves, the surgical kind, and face masks."
Could it be a case of exaggeration?
No. Yes.
Mothers do exaggerate for reasons.

ONE DAY, I had to entertain my very bored baby brother. I took a pair of surgical white gloves, and, with a black marker, I made faces on the fingers. When the gloves wore my hands, my fingertips carried every emotion in the land, and my brother, he was laughter.

MY MOTHER CALLS me from Pakistan. "Soniah, *meri jaan*, stock up on disposable gloves, the surgical kind, and face masks."
Could it be a case of exaggeration?
No. Yes.
Mothers do exaggerate.

I USED THE surgical gloves to henna-dye my black hair a fierce red, the gold-green henna powder mixed with rich brown chai water, my gloved fingers sinking into the quicksand of cool sludge which peaked between my white-hill knuckles; my hair turned into crimson sun, and the gloves stained glass sunflower yellow.

MY MOTHER CALLS me from Pakistan. "Soniah, *meri jaan*, stock up on disposable gloves, the surgical kind, and face masks."
Could it be a case of exaggeration?
No. Yes.
Mothers.

*

I wore a mask when I went into the operating theater to watch my cousin give birth via C-section. I don't know why I wanted to do that. I was allowed to do that because my mother asked for special permission. She warned me that it would be gory. It was. The scalpel sliced through skin, flesh, fat. I almost fainted; I am proud to this day that I did not. The baby was blue and crying, and he slowly turned pink like boiling shrimp. I disliked wearing the mask. It was suffocating. I asked my mother how she could wear it for hours, and she said, "You get used to it."

My mother calls me from Pakistan. "Soniah, *meri jaan*, stock up on disposable gloves, the surgical kind, and face masks."
Could it be a case of exaggeration?
No. Yes.
Mother.

Another time I needed disposable gloves was when I burned my face while cooking. I had never stepped into a kitchen to cook meals in Pakistan, but in America, this is my place. I forced open a whistling pressure cooker and aloo gosht flew at me like fists, the gobs of meat and potatoes and spices and oil holding my face in a heated embrace; it took an hour to call 911. My spectacles are the reason I'm not blind. I was sent home with surgical gloves and Aquaphor, a thick transparent ointment that was to be a barrier between germs in the air and my food-kissed face.

My mother calls me from Pakistan. "Soniah, *meri jaan*, stock up on disposable gloves, the surgical kind, and face masks."
Could it be a case of exaggeration?
No. Yes.

*

My brother comes to visit, and he takes out a pair of surgical white gloves, and, with a black marker, he makes faces on the fingers, and when he wears the gloves to entertain my children, his fingertips carry every emotion in the land, and when my children laugh, I smell love.

My mother calls me from Pakistan. "Soniah, *meri jaan*, stock up on disposable gloves, the surgical kind, and face masks."
    Could it be a case of exaggeration?
    No.

I'm on a too-quick visit to my hometown, Lahore, to launch *An Isolated Incident* at a literary festival. A friend calls to ask if I have time to go on a biking group trip through the streets—Ferozpur Rd., Barkat Market, Kalma Chowk Underground, Cavalry, etc.... When I was growing up, such an excursion used to be a dream, because women biking on streets wasn't done. I make time. I get up early, early. Comfortable clothes. Sneakers. Water. Snack. My mother says, "Don't forget to wear the mask." We cycle through cars, rickshaws, bullock carts, motorbikes, traffic lights, herds of goats. We pedal up inclines and soar back down. Some roads are wide and leafy and paved. Others are narrow and unpaved zigzags of dirt and dust. We wear masks when we need to, but when we talk to each other, we slip them off, "Buck up, come on, faster, slower, a left here, a right here," our mouths coming close, close, the breath of words roaming over our faces, free, free.

My mother calls me from Pakistan. "Soniah, *meri jaan*, stock up on disposable gloves, the surgical kind, and face masks."
    Could it be a case of exaggeration?

*

I OFTEN CARRY disposable gloves when I travel, an old habit instilled by my mother when I was an international student who could get stuck in airports with dirty toilets. In April, I go to Dallas for an *Unmarriageable* event, and from there head to a writer's conference in San Antonio, and from there take a bus to Austin for another *Unmarriageable* event, and, on the bus, I put the gloves to use. I was supposed to have headed to Houston, but I'd been away from home for too long. I wish I hadn't canceled the event in Houston: I would have visited one more Texas city, had I known this might be the end of events for who-on-earth-knows-for-how-long. I board the plane back to Atlanta. At the conference, I purchased a copy of *Sharp: The Women Who Made Art of Having an Opinion*. I open it to the preface. The flight attendant with a complimentary drinks cart asks if I'd like a beverage of my choice, and after she hands me my tomato juice in a plastic cup with a paper napkin around it, she attends across the aisle and asks the aisle seat if he would like a beverage of his choice. He wants alcohol and, yes, he has a credit card, and it is done, and may he have three packets of salted pretzels. Next to him are the two people on the packed flight who are wearing heavy-duty black rubber masks, sitting together, middle seat and window, watching in-flight entertainment. They refuse the offer of a beverage.

MY MOTHER CALLS me from Pakistan. "Soniah, *meri jaan*, also stock up on spray disinfectants and wipes. Have your face masks come? Tuck the mask under your spectacles, tightly, tightly, then they won't fog up. Your spectacles will prevent the virus from entering through your eyes. Yes, it can enter through eyes. No, it can't enter through ears, because ear skin is thick. Make sure to cover mouth and nose. Just keep a distance and nothing will enter from anywhere."

Could it be a case...

*

NOT A DAY goes by when I don't wish someone—even strangers—
on social media my deepest condolences on their loss and a prayer
for the deceased to rest in peace. I wish I'd gone to Houston. I wish
I'd met up with my friends when hugs were hello and hugs were
goodbye. I wish I'd attended the Jewish Muslim Sisterhood coffee
morning after all. I could have made it back in time for my bookstore reading—why didn't I go? I would have greeted all my sisters
with kisses on cheeks and been greeted likewise in turn, and we
would have leaned close into each other, our laughter connecting
our lips. I wish I'd attended the voter registration training at Samad
Mediterranean Grill. Why did I let a migraine stop me? Why did
I take it for guaranteed that there would be a next one and that I'd
just go then? I wish I'd belly danced at Café Istanbul one last time.
I wish I'd taken my kids to dance with me. I wish I'd spent that last
Saturday browsing at the bookstore. I wish I'd spent Sunday at the
bookstore, too. I wish I'd gathered my kids and their friends and
taken them to the park. We would have taken Sultan-Golden to
the dog park, too, where, the loner that he is—like me—he sits and
basks in a wealth of strangers. I wish I'd gone more to write at cafés
and ordered too many coffees and too much cake. I wish I'd gone
yet again to the grocery store and wandered wide-eyed and open-
mouthed through the aisles, like children at zoos. The last film I saw
in the cinema was *Knives Out*. Would I have chosen differently, had
I known? Would I have watched *Thappad* instead? Would I have
watched both back-to-back and thrown in a third, a fourth, a fifth,
a sixth, a seventh, an eighth? When would I have left the building?
I wish to enter crowded elevators and shake hands with all. I wish
I'd eaten at Chaba Thai one last time, but I thought there was next
Tuesday, and next Tuesday, and next Tuesday, and all the Tuesdays
to come. How many hugs and bookstores and films and how much
activism and eating out would it take to say "Now I can do without"?
Then, I told my mother that she was exaggerating and there would

be no need for surgical gloves and masks, let alone a shortage. She may as well have been telling me to stock up on toilet paper, that there would be a run on toilet paper, that the news channels around the world would show America on TV fighting, shouting, hitting, pushing each other out of the way over toilet rolls.

I still wear lipstick even under my mask, and manicured fingers grace my gloves.

My mother calls me from Pakistan, and this time, when she reminds me to stock up on everything, I do. I ask her to take care and stay safe. I tell her I miss her. I miss her. I do not exaggerate.

◇◇

(This essay was first published in the October 2020 issue of *Pithead Chapel*.)

EMILY CARPENTER

Sally Carter

WHEN I'M FINALLY RELEASED FROM THE HOSPITAL AND I go outside, I'm shocked to find April has become June. It is punishingly hot and unbearably humid. Full-on summer in glorious Georgia. After I make the mental adjustment, remind myself how much time I've lost, I realize I'm actually happy. After all, summer is my favorite season.

My house—*our* house—is a small dark-green shingled bungalow with white trim in Decatur, just off the square, that was built in the early 1900s. Today, the sidewalk that leads to it is a treacherous stretch of blazing concrete. Already, a few intrepid earthworms that wriggled out from the grass in the cool morning have been baked, mid-slither, into dark reddish-brown carcasses. I gingerly step over them. Poor things. I expect that this morning, in the brief cool of dawn, they had no idea what the future held for them.

I, on the other hand, know exactly what awaits me. Hearth. Home.

Evan.

And even if we're still in lockdown, even if we can only go for walks and watch TV and pick up food from the restaurants' curbside service, even if we have to finish the tedious task of packing up this house to move, I can't think of anyplace I'd rather be. I wonder if he's been able to keep up with his students and their lessons. There are so many things I lost track of when I was in the hospital.

I push open the white picket gate and head up the walk. The yard looks good, if a bit crunchy from the heat. But the grass is cut and the beds are freshly mulched. Between visits to the hospital, Evan must've done quite a bit of yard work. In fact, I can't remember the last time the place has ever looked this trim.

The front door is red and it's open. Unlocked, I mean. Which is odd. Evan should be at work. I'm glad he's working. I could walk home, and there was no need for a fuss. There's been enough fuss the past two months, with me being sick. With the hospital and the intensive care. Now I appreciate the quiet.

The house is cool and dim, and there are a bunch of glasses of half-drunk Cherry Coke lying around the living room. There are also some grease-stained takeout bags from Five Guys. I make a face but don't tidy up. Evan hates when I clean up after him. "You're not my mother," he says. "You're my partner." He's always been cool that way. He also won't let me do laundry for him, but I suspect that's because I don't fold his T-shirts the way he likes.

When we bought the house, he kept telling me it was haunted. Which I found hilarious, because my husband is such a literalist. He has no interest in supernatural stories, either in movie or book form. He can barely even deal with Halloween. But he says the first time we stepped over the threshold, he felt the presence of a spirit. A benevolent one, he said, who must've died long ago.

The next month, he did some research at the local library. The house, it turned out, was built by a family by the name of Carter whose father was a banker and who had three children. After the children grew up and moved out, the mother and father died, sometime in 1940s. The house sat empty for a while after that—years, I believe. Evan told me he found a note in the documents filed at the courthouse. "Apparently, the son had refused to put the house on the market until after he'd had a medium bless the place."

He folded his arms triumphantly, like I'd told him he'd won the last brownie in the pan. He was right. Our house was haunted.

Nobody's here now. I wander into the kitchen, where all the lights are off, as well, and stand at the breakfast bar. The room's clean, mostly. Just a few dishes in the sink, counters wiped down, and the fridge covered in get-well cards people must've sent me. I've never read them, because they wouldn't let Evan come to the hospital and outside items—cards, flowers, anything—were strictly forbidden.

For some reason, I still don't want to read them. Maybe it's that I'm not sick now. Why go back to that horrible time? That terrifying dream-world of fever and pain where I was never quite sure if I was awake or asleep, drugged or dreaming?

Before lockdown, before I got sick, we decided to sell the house. We'll still do it, I'm pretty sure. I'm not pregnant, not yet, but I plan to be, and our plan was to move north, to Roswell, to be close to my parents, who have basically arranged their retirement around having a grandchild. It took a minute for me to get used to the idea of giving up the in-town life—giving in to that provincial, prosaic suburban life—but Evan was persuasive. He showed me the back-yard that could be ours, a huge sloping expanse of grass bordered by crepe myrtles and azaleas and day lilies, and I was sold. What was more, we'd sell our place in a snap. In Decatur, historic homes that are as well-preserved as ours are always in demand.

That was what I spent most of lockdown doing—when I wasn't on the umpteenth video call, waving like a maniac to officemates I used to barely acknowledge in the days prior to the pandemic. I sorted through all our junk, dividing it into the "brings me joy" or "gives me anxiety" piles. I built up a little wall of boxes in the dining room. There were books in them, many of my childhood favorites and some old journals I used to keep in college. A scrapbook of concert stubs and notes from friends and old emails I printed out when Evan and I used to email.

Now, though, the wall of boxes is gone.

Where…?

I glance around the kitchen and then venture into the hallway. They're not here, either. Maybe Evan's put them in storage. Or taken them up to Mom and Dad's house. They have a basement as well as an extra room for the grandchild who will hopefully soon be conceived. But I don't know. The not knowing makes me anxious. I would like to see the boxes.

I hear a sound. A door banging closed. I realize Evan was back in the garage, a narrow little one-car relic crammed between the fence and the tiny patio out back that he uses as a recording studio. Probably his footsteps make a *slap, slap, slap* across the patio, getting louder as he nears the house, and I don't know why, but I'm suddenly seized with the urge to hide. I only intended to surprise him, not scare him, but suddenly I'm not ready. I'm second-guessing my plan, and so, to buy myself more time, I scoot down the hall and up the narrow steps that lead to the attic.

It's dim, lit only by the light coming in one small window, but it's clean. My neurotic pandemic cleaning reached all the way up here, and I spent two full days clearing clutter, dusting, and even mopping. There is the odd chair and lamp we couldn't fit downstairs but we're not ready to give away. But the boxes, my boxes, aren't up here, either.

I hear the backdoor slam, there's a pause, and then music fills the house. When I hear what it is, it makes me smile. Nina Simone is one of my favorites. Evan leans more toward country, not this kind of soul, especially the more political stuff. So there is something touching, something especially sweet, about my husband listening to my music when I'm not here. The feeling is so unexpected that my throat seems to swell, and I feel like I can't catch my breath. I put my hand on my chest to calm myself.

I'm not sick anymore.

It's over.

But still I think I might cry.

"Do you live here?" someone behind me asks in a quiet voice.

I turn. It's a little girl, six or seven, standing by the one small window. She's standing just outside of the shaft of light, so she's mostly doused in shadow, but I can see she's got light brown hair that hangs in soft curls and she's wearing a short, shapeless dress. Her feet are bare. This is not all that unusual, finding children in my home. Evan teaches music to children from five to eighteen, and there's basically not any time there's not some child sitting in our living room banging on our piano, sawing away on a violin, or strumming a slow-motion song on a guitar. He must be back to the lessons. I'm glad.

"Does Evan know you're here?" I say, hoping not to scare her. "Where are your shoes?"

"I'm not sure," she says, and I wonder which question she's answering. I decide to start over.

"What do you play?"

"Piano," she says.

I nod. Evan's original instrument. I bet he likes this kid. He likes the little ones. The teens drive him nuts. Too cool for school. Even Evan's music school, which is pretty cool.

"Have you already had your lesson?" I ask.

She nods but looks a little unsure.

"Maybe we ought to head down," I say encouragingly. Her mom will be pissed if she finds out she only got thirty minutes instead of the forty-five that she paid for. But the girl withdraws further into the shadows.

I stop. "Is this your first lesson?"

No answer.

"Are you new?" I ask the question as gently as I can, hoping she's not a crier.

"No, *you're* new," she says.

This jolts me. I cock my head. Smile. But that throat-constricting thing comes back.

"I've been sick," I say. My voice sounds high and uncertain. I wonder why.

She nods. "I was sick, too."

"Oh. I'm sorry to hear that."

She shrugs, and for some reason I think of the earthworms. Not flash frozen, but flash baked. They had no idea, did they? None of us do. And an attic can be a sidewalk can be a hospital bed. This makes me think of a question I want to ask, but as soon as it occurs to me, it slips away again, and my mind is a blank. No matter. I move to the top of the stairs. Nina Simone's lush, deep voice lifts up to us. She is singing about spells.

"Evan," I call down. "Someone's here."

No answer comes.

"Evan," I yell again. "It's a student!"

The music must be too loud. I want to go downstairs, but I know I'll definitely startle him. Now I'm feeling strange. Out of place in my own house.

Where are my boxes?

I feel something behind me—wave of cool air—and I turn to find the little girl standing beside me. My skin goes to goosebumps, but when I look down, it's so dark I can barely see the outline of my own arms. They are thin, I think. Too thin. I should eat. I need meat on my bones.

"He's been playing that for days," the girl says. Her voice sounds dreamy.

My mouth drops open. "You've been up here for days? We really should call your mother."

She nods. "I did. But she moved away." She brightens. "But I think he'll stay. That's what he told the lady who came by the other day." She takes another step toward me. "He wants to stay. Isn't that nice?"

I know. The whole time she's talking, I know what's going on, but I don't want to say it out loud. Saying it out loud makes it true. Saying it out loud brings back the fever and the cough and the drowning and the blackness. The fear and the loneliness.

I was so alone then. All alone, right up to the end. That was not how it was supposed to be. Evan was supposed to be there, but he wasn't, so that's probably why now all I can think about is how I don't want to be separated from him anymore.

"I know," the girl says. And she does know, I can tell. She knows a lot. A lot more than me.

"Do we have to stay up here? In the attic?" I ask her, but before she can answer, I hear the door to the attic stairs bang against the wall.

"Is somebody there?" Evan calls up. The girl presses one finger to her mouth.

I hear his feet on the steps, heavy thudding that doesn't sound at all like the upbeat, lighthearted, light-on-his-feet Evan I know. He's coming up. Both of us, the girl and I, back into separate corners of the attic like a strange dance we automatically know the steps to, and in a few seconds, Evan reaches the top of the stairs. When I catch sight of his messy dark-blond hair and serious face, I am overcome. I nearly rush toward him so I can wrap my arms around him. Kiss him and bury my face in his neck. But I don't because I know it wouldn't do me any good. Then I notice he is sweating, and I think, of course he is; it's June. But I am not. I am cool. Too cool for school.

"Sally Carter," Evan says into the emptiness of the attic. His voice is reverent, the voice of an acolyte, and the name sounds like an incantation.

I start to answer him—*No, it's me*—but the little girl puts her hand out to stop me.

"I'm here," she says aloud toward Evan.

Evan straightens, as though he's heard her but doesn't quite recognize from which direction her voice is coming. "Is she here?" he asks, his voice soft, earnest. "Have you seen her?" He's looking up into the ceiling. I almost want to laugh now, but I want to cry, too. There are too many conflicting emotions inside me. So much longing that I don't know where to put it. I long to laugh. Laugh this off as a joke. But that won't make it not real. And maybe it will scare him. I don't want to scare him. I need him. I need him so desperately.

The little girl looks very grave. "She's here with me now."

She touches my thin, cool arm, and I let out a gasp. At the same time, Evan does, too, but even then, he doesn't look in my direction. He only covers his mouth with his hands as tears fill his eyes.

"Evan," I say softly.

The girl turns to me, a warning hand out. "Not yet," she says quietly. "But soon, I promise. It's not easy to reach them. Sometimes the things you think are louder than what you say."

"I don't understand," I whisper.

"This used to be my house. I left in 1918—after I was sick—but I came back, just like you, later on. It took some time before I could reach my mother, but I worked hard and I did it. I'll teach you how, too, if you'd like."

I stare at her.

"It's good that he believes," she adds. "And he's not moving any-more. There'll be time. That's really good. It takes time."

I look back at my husband—my dear sweet husband, who's de-cided to stay in the house where he lived with his wife who died sometime in early May, *Yes, it was early May,* I think—and with every ounce of power I have within me, I will him to look at me. To see me. But he doesn't. He just turns as though to head back down the stairs again. But after one step down, he stops, his hand on the rail. He turns back, his face transformed into an expression of wonder mixed with anguish. He still is looking past me.

"I put the boxes in your closet," he says quietly to the empty attic, and then he descends the rest of the way down the stairs, back into our house.

CLAYTON H. RAMSEY

Savannah, 1876

D R. WILLIAM BEAUREGARD STEPHENS TOLERATED NO mawkish sentiment. He had seen too much death and suffering in his practice to allow a tempest of feelings to storm his scientific mind. Not that he was incapable of emotion, just that he controlled it exquisitely. Cool, steady, measured—he was the perfect model of a seasoned medical practitioner.

He was also prominent enough to be on the reviewing stand of one of the grander parades of the centennial celebration of the signing of the Declaration of Independence. The route took the cohorts of bands, soldiers, and social groups down the widest thoroughfare in Savannah. Buildings were festooned in red, white, and blue bunting, streamers and confetti tossed from windows to fill the air with swirling bits of color. There were long-winded addresses by dignitaries, prayers of gratitude from eminent clergy for a century of divine protection. One hundred years of freedom from British control was something that demanded a party. But by the end of the month, when the humidity descended like a thick, sodden quilt and the mosquitoes relentlessly sought salty flesh, vessels arrived from Havana and disease was offloaded with cargo.

It was no surprise that he did not cry at Tabitha's funeral, drawn only by a sense of duty and common decency to the graveyard that day. Instead of the drums and trumpets of the Fourth, there were only the soft words of the preacher and the drone of insects. He stood in an inch of damp, his polished shoes sinking in the spongy ground of the Laurel Grove Cemetery, South, in a patch also known as the Old Negro Cemetery. The tended, lush property with good drainage was confined to Laurel Grove North, reserved for the white residents of this low-country city. Blacks had to settle for eternal rest in inferior plots.

Tabitha had been one of his house servants, cooking, cleaning, and mending, keeping domestic life running while his wife was involved with the ladies' auxiliary at the hospital where he was on staff. Planning cotillions and gathering for tea with the other women of Savannah society did not provide her with either the time or the energy to maintain a household, even if she'd had the interest, which she did not, and so the weight of responsibility had fallen on Tabitha.

Tabitha had lived with her husband, Tommy, in an attic room in the expansive three-story home of the Stephens family. While she'd done housework, he'd served as butler and personal attendant to Dr. Stephens. It had been a complicated arrangement. Dr. Stephens's father had been the owner of a lucrative plantation in the rice fields that surrounded the city. By exploiting slave labor, he had built a fortune that had catapulted the family into the rarefied world of Savannah privilege and allowed them to send their only son to study medicine in Philadelphia at a time when those of lesser resources could only learn the trade by apprenticing with a local physician. William had been fortunate in that respect, and many others.

The elder Stephens had bought Tommy, his parents, and his younger sister when William had been a teenager. Tommy had become a house slave for the family, invisible, always available but never noticed. At least he hadn't been in the malarial rice swamps with the other field hands, fighting the heat, insects, snakes, and crushing physical demands of outdoor work. But it had still been demeaning. After Sherman had burned his way to Savannah, everything had changed. Lincoln had liberated the slaves but had blasted the economic machinery of the South. William had had his education and little else. Tommy had had his freedom, but that had not been quite enough. William had hired him as a freedman when everything else had gone to hell.

Tommy was glad he was not in a northern factory or toiling as a sharecropper, but working for the man whose family had used to own him perpetuated his sense of dependency and fueled his anger. He was emancipated but not free, and that tension stirred a stew of resentment and pain that threatened to spill over into every minute he stayed with Dr. Stephens. But stay he did. Hunger and limited opportunity were powerful motivators.

By August, death had replaced revelry. 1820 had seen it. So had 1854. Now, in 1876, yellow fever had slashed its way back to their city and was tearing through the population. White residents of means boarded trains and steamboats and fled the pestilence. Those without, the poor and most freedmen, stayed. Many doctors, faithful to their Oath, remained as well. Tabitha had been one of the few blacks Dr. Stephens had known who had succumbed to the disease. Whites were more likely to be victims of the fever, many suffering the jaundice, shock, internal bleeding, and black vomit of those at the end stages of the illness. So if they had the chance to flee before they caught it, they did. Dr. Stephens had sent his wife and two daughters to Atlanta by rail to stay with an aunt and uncle of his. Tommy had soon been a widower.

By the end of the month, when the Board of Health in Savannah finally acknowledged the extent of the disease and the threat it posed, there was only Dr. Stephens and Tommy in the cavernous home. Tommy was almost swallowed whole by grief, and Dr. Stephens yearned to be with his family. There was no company between them, only two men sharing the same space but living in two universes of pain and longing.

With an early spring and incessant rainfall, the first case of yellow fever had appeared in Savannah by late July and had spread through the estates of the wealthy and the neighborhoods of the less affluent. Neat columns in the *Savannah Morning News* had reported the mortality records of the day before. Life in the city had changed. Businesses had lost customers who had either fled the city or were afraid to venture beyond their front doors. Streets had emptied. City resources, already stretched thin as officials speculated on future commercial ventures to rival the emerging prominence of Atlanta after the War, had become even scarcer for citizens in need. Public services had been less reliable, but benevolent societies had stepped up, trying to fill in the gaps with food and clothes. Families had been separated by death, or split by necessity, like the Stephenses. As the weeks ticked off the calendar, undertakers worked overtime to bury all the bodies. This microscopic virus had shifted the rhythms of the entire city. The niceties of civilization were stripped away, seen as inessential, leaving only the raw struggle for survival among those who remained.

For Dr. Stephens and Tommy, their lives collapsed onto a pinpoint focus; the doctor attended the sick and dying, and Tommy attended him. There were no galas, no medical conferences, no trips out of town for the former, and no time away to fish or Sunday services for the latter. Life changed for both of them, and that life revolved around home visits and hospital visits and doing everything to keep those visits possible.

The schedule was the same every day for both of them. Both would awake at dawn. Clean, shave, dress. Then Tommy would make a couple of hardboiled eggs, toast, and black coffee for both of them. The full board had disappeared with Tabitha. Dr. Stephens would eat his in the dining room at the end of a long mahogany table, with silver that had lost its luster. The other end was usually occupied by his wife, his two girls between them, and the absence of the three made him ache as he ate his Spartan meal and scanned the news. Tommy ate in the kitchen. Even though there was only the two of them, eating together would have been unseemly, a violation of social custom.

They soon developed a routine that did not require words. Dr. Stephens would take his medical bag from his study and his hat from the rack next to the grandfather clock in the foyer. He did not wear the long leather coat and beak-and-goggle hood of seventeenth-century plague physicians, but he was nevertheless identified as a medic by his bag and dark suit at a time when other professionals had already fled. By the time he turned the key in the front door, he expected Tommy to have hitched the horse to the buggy and be waiting for him at the curb. Tommy usually had fifteen minutes after the end of breakfast to prepare the ride. Their first stop was the hospital for rounds on the wards, increasingly filled with victims of the fever. In more pleasant times, Dr. Stephens would go to his surgery and see patients who had made an appointment with him. He would inspect rashes, hear accounts of intestinal disturbances, sometimes set a broken bone. Now the need was so overwhelming that he went from house to house, seeing dozens by the end of the day. Fever, chills, fatigue, nausea, vomiting, body aches. There was no variety from patient to patient. At least those had some hope of recovery. For the less fortunate who did not recover from this stage of the malaise, there was only the inevitability of an excruciating death. Dr. Stephens tried to ease their pain. Some he bled, others he gave purgatives. He tried mercury and mustard poultices. Although he would never admit it, he felt helpless on most days, overwhelmed by a disease that had no mercy and no cure.

Tommy waited for him in the buggy at every stop. All he saw were the façades of lovely homes of sick white people. None of the stops were shanties, none on the edge of town. He saw a society doctor taking care of his own. This was what circulated in his mind day after day. All he did was think; he had no one to talk to. He had heard chewing garlic kept the fever away, so he always had a clove in his cheek, chewing and thinking and seething. As unpleasant as the garlic was, he didn't want to die the way he saw every day.

Between stops, Dr. Stephens would pull a handkerchief dipped in vinegar from a little leather pouch he kept in the cab to clear his passages of the miasma of death that had settled on the city. He had never been much of a cigar smoker, but he became one. Disease came through the air—the best medical authorities believed it—and so he wanted to kill off the microbes and keep them from settling in his body.

By the time they returned home after dark, their clothes stank of the smoke that filled the streets from fires set in the squares. Exhausted, Dr. Stephens would retreat to his study for a brandy. Every afternoon, a local woman was paid to bring a basket of food for both of them and would leave it on the stoop. While Dr. Stephens caught his breath, Tommy unpacked the provisions and put his employer's fare on clean china and left it for him in the dining room. His portion was consumed in the kitchen. Sometimes Dr. Stephens would read after dinner, answer correspondence, write medical reports on the activities of the day.

After cleaning up, Tommy would go to his room in the attic. He liked to carve little figurines out of hunks of Georgia pine, and sometimes he would. Usually he just fell into bed. Before he drifted off to sleep, he would think of Tabitha, of the song she would sing to him every morning, of the sparkle of her smile. Some nights it was more than he could bear. Dr. Stephens never talked to him, and the routine never changed. He knew his job and he did it. But without Tabitha, there were no dreams, no conversation, no person to share his hopes and hardships. He had thoughts, plenty of them, not that Dr. Stephens cared. He was a driver, a cook, a Man Friday, not a human being who yearned and suffered and imagined a life beyond the small circle that existence had become. Sharing a building with this man, he was nevertheless completely alone. Dr. Stephens had his own life, his own concerns for the health of the city—Tommy understood that—but it didn't make their shared life any easier. They might just as well have occupied different planets spinning independently in the same galaxy.

And so it went until one stormy night.

Tommy was in his garret when he heard the jingle of the front doorbell, followed by the first word Dr. Stephens had spoken to him in weeks.

"Tommy!" he shouted to the ceiling.

Tommy pulled on his pants and slipped on his boots as he stumbled down the stairs and into the foyer to confront an absolutely improbable scene. His employer was standing on the threshold, wrapped in a housecoat cinched at the waist. Before him was a wisp of a black girl, her frayed cotton dress stuck to her slim body by rainwater, rain dripping from the dark curls of her hair onto the pale blue planks of the front porch.

"Please come," was all the girl said, over and over, her tiny hand reaching for the hem of Dr. Stephens's robe. "Mama needs help."

Tommy was assaulted with questions. Who was this girl? Who was her mother? What was she doing showing up at the Stephens home at this hour and in this storm? If she had been white, he would have had the same questions. But because she was not, he had many more.

"Tommy, hitch up the buggy. I'll change and grab my bag. Be waiting for me on the street." Tommy knew the routine, but this was a different class of patient. Still, he bit his tongue. Now was not the time for questions, only action.

He bundled the girl into the cab with the doctor before he vaulted into the driver's seat and snapped the reins on the slick back of the horse. They tore through the streets as Tommy strained to see through the lashing rain and hear directions in the girl's thin voice over the clatter of the buggy wheels and whip of the storm. They passed through the downtown business district, through neighborhoods that mapped out a slide down the economic scale. Square by square, they made their way across the city. Closer in were the houses of judges, lawyers, politicians, most shuttered and dark. The farther they drove, the more people and light they saw in houses that were more dilapidated, filled with day laborers, dock workers, and those who propped up the city with their unseen efforts.

On the periphery of town, the landscape was marshy, and the muddy, rutted roads slowed their progress until they reached a shanty set back in a copse of trees. The girl and the doctor leapt from the cab and ran into the shack. Tommy stood in the rain, listening as it hit the leaves high up in the trees and fell onto the corrugated tin roof of the modest structure. Five, ten, twenty minutes passed. And then Dr. Stephens emerged, his shirtsleeves pushed up to his elbows. He quietly wiped his hands, unrolled his sleeves, replaced his hat, and plodded back to the buggy.

"Let's go home, Tommy," he said.

By the time they returned to the Stephens residence, the rain had subsided. There was a heavy calm in the air that followed the storm. Dr. Stephens went to his room, as Tommy did to his. They nodded to each other when they parted, a polite gesture without words, acknowledging their day was over before it started again a few hours of rest later.

The next morning, Dr. Stephens did not appear in the dining room for breakfast. Tommy thought he was sleeping a few extra hours after a late night. He didn't show for lunch or dinner, either. Perhaps he was taking the day off, Tommy thought. Maybe he had snuck away for the day, spent it with friends. But Tommy knew he had no such luxury as the fever continued to sweep through the city.

As the sun slipped below the horizon, Tommy gently knocked on the door of Dr. Stephens's bedroom. No response. He pressed his ear against the door. No sound. He eased the door open a crack. He saw the doctor on his bed, sound asleep. He had been working hard, and it had been wet and chilly the night before. Maybe it was just a cold. Maybe simple exhaustion. He would let him rest. He did not want to imagine what was beginning.

The morning after the storm, Dr. Stephens could feel the warmth in his body, the slow burn of fever. He hoped it was early-stage influenza, but he feared worse. When he was not sweating with the febrile heat, he was shivering. He called for blankets, for the coals in his bedroom brazier to be stoked, if only for a moment, to end the teeth-rattling chill. But his voice didn't reach beyond his room. His whole world was now defined by the boundaries of his mattress. The progressive constriction of his life, from distinguished society doctor surrounded by colleagues, patients, and family to lone plague physician trying to keep what remained of his city from collapsing, was now almost complete as he became an isolated patient, utterly abandoned. His thoughts, once so ordered, so logical, shimmered like a desert mirage. He could feel himself sinking into ache and bone-weariness, hot sweat and cold sweat binding him even more securely to his little island of pain.

In more lucid moments, he remembered his wife and girls, cried out for them. But they were gone. Tabitha had passed. And Tommy? Where was Tommy? Dr. Stephens couldn't sit up, couldn't communicate his needs. His only prayer was that this man he shared his house with would somehow decide to come to him, help him, save him. He couldn't make that happen. For the first time in his life, he realized he was completely dependent on another. Dr. Stephens's money, influence, and position couldn't force Tommy through the door. But that was his only hope. He had no idea what Tommy was doing, just that he was absent. Would there be any relief?

Days passed. Tommy didn't want to disturb the doctor's much-needed rest, but he suspected there might be a problem. For Dr. Stephens, the days were long and the nights longer. Tommy finally slipped into Dr. Stephens's room in the cool of twilight. Dr. Stephens was moaning softly, tangled in sheets. Tommy reached out and touched his forehead. Unnaturally warm. Tommy retraced his steps back into the hall, pulling the door closed until he heard the click of the latch bolt. In a few strides, he was in the front sitting room, and there he started to pace. The more he paced, the more anxious he became. *What is wrong? Is this yellow fever? What do I do? Dr. Stephens is the man others came to for help. With him sick, who do I go to?* He did laps around the red velvet couch. He wasn't used to making his own decisions. *Think.* He didn't know how to treat yellow fever. He didn't know what to do. *Pace. Think.*

And then a thought slithered into his agitated mind. Maybe this had been divinely engineered to provide an escape for Tommy. He could walk away from this house that had become his prison. He could step into the world. No more *Yes sir, no sir, may I have permission to blow my nose, sir.* This was his opportunity. He was no slave; he could leave. He could smash some china, drive a kitchen knife into some upholstery, slip a couple of silver candlesticks into his pockets, and march into what lay beyond the confines of this house. All the rage over injustices he had suffered his entire life lit a fire under the cauldron of his mind, and hope bubbled up. He could leave, start over, take what he wanted, and go.

In his pacing, he walked into the dining room and up to the sideboard. Pulled a fat cigar from the humidor, fired it up, dropped into the chair Dr. Stephens usually occupied during meals, and threw his feet up on the sacrosanct mahogany table. As he smoked and thought, the more warmly he entertained the idea of smashing, grabbing, and fleeing. He had every right. He worked hard, but he had nothing. He and his family had been slaves. Now was his time to taste true freedom.

The grandfather clock in the foyer chimed, and it was as though the sound dissolved his feverish dream. Where would he go? How would he survive? Would he be forced into even more unpleasant and restrictive circumstances just to eat? Would men who were not patient with lawbreakers of his color track him down for destruction of property, theft, maybe even murder? And what would Tabitha say about his plan? She had dragged him to services at the Baptist church every Sunday when she'd been alive. How was this loving your neighbor? How was this not breaking commandments? The laws of God and man shouted in his conscience, and they were answered with a scream of rage that had been stoked by years of pain. He was tingling with emotion and conflicting desires.

Until he felt a light hand on his shoulder and a cool breath whisper in his ear. *Help him*, she said. He turned, half-expecting to see his one love behind him. He was by himself, but for the first time in months, he didn't feel alone. He would be the better man. He snuffed out the cigar and found a bowl for water and a hand towel in the kitchen. He spent the rest of the day and the days that followed trying to ease the suffering of Dr. Stephens, wiping his brow, tipping a glass of water to his lips, holding his head as he vomited, retrieving medicines.

The fever did eventually break, sparing Dr. Stephens from the gruesome end of many of his patients. His slow emergence from the grip of illness was matched by a developing and unexpected sense of gratitude to Tommy. Prior to this episode, Tommy had been an employee whose attention had been required. *Why should you be thankful to someone who was simply doing his job*, Dr. Stephens had thought. But now that his life had been saved by a man whose ministrations had not been commanded but given as a gift of pure compassion, his perspective shifted. As for Tommy, he now saw Dr. Stephens as a man, a fragile human being who got sick and needed help. His white skin, his medical degree, his affluence, once such defining characteristics of his assumed superiority, now seemed less important than his simple humanity, assailable by the same diseases and frailties that afflicted every other person, Tommy included. Though neither wanted to admit it, the fever had created a subtle leveling of their relationship.

Mrs. Stephens returned with their girls after the first frost of the year, and nothing more was said about their time together until, one afternoon, Dr. Stephens called Tommy into his study.

"Tommy, I'm not a perfect man," he began. "I've tried to be a good doctor, a good husband, a good father. And I want to do good by you. In addition to being faithful to me and my family for so many years, you also saved my life." A drop formed in the corner of his eye.

Tommy sat paralyzed in front of him. He had never seen a hint of emotion in Dr. Stephens as long as he had known him.

"I can never really repay you for what you've done for me, but I want to try."

Tommy nodded almost imperceptibly.

"I want to teach you to read, and then I want to teach you what I know about medicine. You can still maintain your employment here until you've learned what you need to know to be out on your own."

Now it was Tommy's turn to be misty-eyed.

"The woman I treated before I got sick was the daughter of my nursemaid growing up. I loved her as much as I did my own mother. But what I can do for her family is limited. I hope, as a healer, you can help her and many like her. I want you to live the life you want. You probably won't be invited to join the Savannah Medical Society yet, but you will be able to live a life on your terms, not mine. And maybe together, we can make some changes in this old world. This is the best gift I know to give you. I only wish I could do more."

Tommy swiped his eyes with his sleeve and stuck out his hand. William met it with his and they shook, for the first time as men. William had his family and Tommy his freedom, never again alone together in Georgia.

TARA WHITE

Humming

Alone in Atlanta
A walk in the trees
The slow Chattahoochee
Wild grass to my knees

With all my acquaintance
Still shuttered away
The hot thriving virus
The toll that we pay

A sudden opossum
Skitters right 'cross my path
And there a swift sparrow
Splashing a bath

Glossy black racer snakes
Track near the dock
And paper-white egrets
On an islet of rock

Stand stiff on straw legs
I blink and they move
While chipmunks and squirrels
Unearth buried food

From Georgia red clay
Red dust on my shoes
The thrumming of bumblebees
Sharing bee news

A spindle-legged family
Of deer, heads bowed low
They startle and quick bolt
With lithe fawns in tow

Then twilight at solstice
Blue hours in between
Conjure murmurs of barn owls
Heard but not seen

No near soul to share this
Bright halcyon day
Just all the Earth's creatures
Humming away

DAVID FULMER

And a Clown's Farewell

THE LOCAL COMES TO A GRUDGING, GRINDING HALT AT THE 13th Street station and stalls, motionless, in one of the endless delays for which the system is famous. It seems, at times, as though there's been a sudden decision to abandon the entire concept of mass rail transit as unworkable, and trains such as this one have been left to run down to rust while unwitting riders, having paid their fares, sit waiting for a conductor who will never arrive.

Passengers like Stanley Mach, precisely the sort of trusting soul who will linger there until the sun blinks out and the moon dies a blue death, convinced to the end that the wheels will turn and the journey into the dirty heart of the city will resume.

So Stanley, a quiet man of thirty-nine who is friendly only with his shadow, perches on the torn seat, a flightless bird heading calmly toward extinction while a tattered volume of García Lorca that he bought for fifty cents sits open on his knee.

As he ponders the line *Why was I born among mirrors?* his gaze roams to the northbound platform, and in that instant, he beholds something that halts his breath halfway up his throat. He jerks his eyeballs back to the printed page, but the next lines, *The day walks in circles around me and the night copies me in all its stars…* don't register at all, because there is a busy voice inside his head telling him that for the first time in his life, after nearly forty years, Pee-Wee-League Dante Stanley Mach is witnessing a *bona fide* vision.

She is standing next to one of the heavy steel pillars, arrayed in a ragtag assortment of colors and patterns. Nothing unusual there; it's the fashion of the day, or so Stanley surmises from the glances he steals at the pretty women who enter and exit the stage of his cycle of plays. She wears round, tinted glasses, and a purple beret slouches on dark curls that fall around a face that is the color of ginger and freckled. And, as he lives and breathes, a cloud of pale amber envelops her with such luminance that he is stirred to the sudden conclusion that this is the angel he has heard about, read about, dreamed about for so long.

More likely, he tells himself, she's the final sign that he has lost it for good and that the years of banging punches off the inside of his skull as Stanley Mach, the failed artist, failed husband, failed a-good-bit-more, has knocked him for the kind of permanent loop that will land him next to the fat little man in the corner market who delights in shouting red-faced diatribes at the fresh produce.

And yet, peeking again, she appears to be the very one over whom he has wept and fasted, wept and prayed, and he gapes in absent wonder, thinking, *Here she is after all this time and sonofabitch if I'm not going the wrong way.*

And as though he needs more in the way of a sign, the doors slide open, and now resolved, he closes his book, stands up, and steps onto the platform. Taking a moment to steady his nerves, he makes himself take slow steps to the bottom of the stairs, where he stops, readying to look again and find that she has evaporated into the humid air of the tunnel and from the crooked cavern of his imagination. But when he peers across the tracks, she's still there, a lone figure wrapped in faint light under the great cathedral dome of the station.

So he begins to climb, Stanley explaining to Stanley that all he wants is to see her up close and then travel on, recalling a rainy afternoon years before when he rode a bus all the way to the end of the line because the woman sitting across from him had a sad, sweet light in her eyes. He remembers the ballet of her stepping off the bus and into the arms of the fellow waiting at the stop and that his regret was touched with a faint relief.

Returning to present tense, it occurs to him that not all the trains were frozen like his on the tracks and that he might reach the other side to find that she has whisked away to another deep crevice of the city and into someone else's dream. He starts climbing.

Just as he reaches street-level, a rumbling tells him the Number Three is approaching and that he can now either let the whole matter be swept away by the hot wind of the departing train or descend the stairs to the other side and perhaps chase a ghost over half the city, only to end up watching her fade into air, proving finally that he has gone plain crazy on the brittle edges of his days and has spun just that much closer to the asylum or the grave with nothing to show for it but aching feet.

He chooses the latter and hurries downward. The train, all *whoosh* and roar and sleek chrome steel, pulls to a stop. She slips into the car nearest the engine and he follows, keeping his distance and settling across from an old man who, at first blush, reminds him so much of his grandfather long-dead that he almost says, "Hey, Pop, you know there's some kind of angel on this train?"

It sounds ridiculous, and when he looks again, he sees that the man isn't so familiar after all, but wears the grim, beaten look that always gives him the creeps, and he rises and moves toward the front of the car. Finding a seat, he looks around and sees that she's gone. Gone. An illusion, of course. What was he thinking? An *angel*, yet?

The train pulls out and he turns to his reflection in the dark window, mulling over his mask for a blank minute before noticing another reflection: hers, floating in black. He turns in slow motion, expecting nothing. But there she sits, not ten feet away, calmly regarding her folded hands. He shifts his gaze. The soft, pulsing light around her hurts his eyes, plus it would be impolite, so he steals glances as he listens to the deep hum of the turbine and the *clack-clack-clack* of the steel wheels so intently that he all but forgets where he is and what he is doing.

Her face is animated by a smile, as though there's a joke echoing in her ears or some slapstick playing before eyes that are an undersea green, eyes that hold him, even after she tilts her head, stands up, and moves to the door. He is aware of the train rolling into a station, the door opening, and her stepping off. Yet he sits like a ventriloquist's dummy, all the words he might have said if and when he ever encountered the mystical flapping out of his mouth in perfect silence. Here's Stanley, making soundless speeches while the only true angel he'll ever see walks away.

Seconds later, a self-administered kick in the ass sends him down the aisle and onto the platform. He catches sight of her heading for the steps and then rising and disappearing. Again.

She's got a good lead, and he huffs upward to the heat and hard smells of a mechanical city. Here, the intersection fans out around the station. He looks left and right, up and down, over a street jammed with hoods and fenders, swelling in a minor symphony of metallic shrieks, coughs, rumbles, whistles, and bleats. For a sudden instant, he hovers, one foot on the curb and the other in midair, before plunging in and crossing over, seeking a telltale flash of light or motion.

Not so fast, Stanley. One of God's self-appointed sales reps steps up to block his path, barking out a litany of distress, despair, damnation, destruction, and death so graphic that if he were a weaker soul, the soon-to-be-forty heathen might break down, smite his head for its vanity, strike his heart for its foolishness, flog his loins for their hopeless lusts, and sign up for salvation right there on the spot.

Instead, he rushes by, already aware that if this gentleman who bellows with such dire eloquence is even half-right, "lost soul" is a major understatement. He catches a glimpse of purple beret disappearing through a doorway to a set of stairs leading—big surprise—downward again.

Into a swamp of heat and smoke and noise, Stanley dives, first to a doorway where a pasty-faced woman is collecting a cover. He pays five dollars to pass inside.

That his angel is not among the few random souls hanging at the edges of the room is, for the moment, of no concern. If this is Hades, he decides, all bets are off, because an electric shiver is shaking the walls and the only agony is coming from the speakers on the wall and the voice of a singer wringing dark passion from her soul like water out of a rag. It's the blues, all right; he knows by the hand reaching down into the pit of his gut, about to drag him away.

It calls for a drink, and he finds his way to the end of the empty bar, waves a hand, puts down some cash, and is rewarded with a cold beer. After draining the glass in three grateful swallows and smacking his lips with the gusto of a steelworker, he lifts it for a refill at the very moment she steps from a shadow, so that it appears to all the world that he has raised his empty vessel in her honor. He stands in this absurd posture until she looks his way and hikes a curious eyebrow, as though she half-remembers him from back when.

Stanley glances over his shoulder, a reflex to locate the handsome sport who is always hanging behind him to collect a stranger's smile. There's no such character in sight, and he turns back, almost convinced that it was meant for him. *Was*, goddamnit, because she's slipped off again, with a little trail of light flitting up the steps behind her. He sags against the bar, thinking as the sweet music throbs that if not for the fact that he's already invested his time, pieces of his heart, and ten dollars for the cover charge and beer, he'd stay right where he is.

Once on the sidewalk, he glances at his watch and is stunned to see that it's past three o'clock. What happened to the hours of the night? Was Einstein correct? Or is time an accordion, and if so, will the universe play "Lady of Spain" or something more in the zydeco vein? He mulls the question until four-wheeled reality pulls to the curb not twenty feet away.

Dumbfounded, Stanley watches her slide into the taxi. Though he's seen this sort of thing only in the movies, he steps to the curb, flags a cab of his own, jumps in, and yells at the driver to *Go! Go!* This earns him a hairy eyeball and something muttered in a heavy accent about *Not want no trouble*. But once he waves a handful of dollars like a sprightly bouquet, the driver grins, grabs the shifter, and launches the vehicle into traffic.

Though the cab is heaving about like a boat on a rough sea, Stanley catches glimpses out the window at parts of the city that have been transformed, wide and bright, spilling color as though from a brush in a cartoon, an electric riot in every gaudy hue on the neon palette. He is frankly amazed. When did it happen? Where has he been? He feels like a coma victim who wakes to find that decades have passed, children are grown, friends dead, landmarks of memory replaced by donut shops and oil-change-and-lube franchises.

A shrieked curse in some arcane tongue jerks him from this rumination, and he looks up in time to see their quarry beat the red light ahead. He moans out loud, but his driver waves him quiet with a chopping hand and flogs the cab across the intersection.

The city hasn't changed so much that he is totally lost. They are heading east along a quieter corridor of small shops and cafés, still part of the old sections he remembers. His driver mutters a steady stream of angry verbiage that goes on until he lets out a sudden yelp of delight, jabs a finger, and swerves to the curb. The other cab has stopped, and she's out and swirling away.

A pleased Stanley produces extra money. He and the driver cackle and smile, trade gibberish. He jumps out, and the cab roars away in a screech of rubber and cloud of white.

And now he stands on the sidewalk in the last remnants of the dusky night, the chase over, for she is captured now, framed and fixed in the window of an all-night diner. From her booth, she stares onto the street, her aura diffused by the cool glow of white neon, looking lonely and innocent and beautiful. Stanley, watching her, senses the first fissures of a breaking heart and steals into a shadow to nurse the wound. From there, he watches a fat old waitress bring her a steaming cup and something on a plate. As she eats and sips and broods, he realizes that his stomach is empty and that he would die for a simple mug of coffee.

She doesn't see him hiding in the darkness, and he forgets where he is until something wet touches his face. The wind lifts and a light rain begins falling as the pale gray fingers of dawn rise over the rooftops to the west. He looks back toward the diner to see that she's left behind nothing but an empty table and some dirty dishes. He draws a breath, the first cool air of morning, and decides that he has reached the end of the line. And about time, too; it's time to find his way home, if he can.

"Why are you following me?"

For a moment, he thinks it's another voice in his head. But when he looks up, she's standing just outside the diner doors, watching him with that same curious expression. He gives a start of sudden alarm that she thinks he's been stalking her with evil intent and is about to yell for a cop. Or giggle her derision. Or smack him. And then run away forever. With all this, he can't summon any words.

"Why are you following me?" she asks again, and instead of fear or annoyance, he hears the soft and amused melody of her voice, like the sound of a dove in flight.

He manages to say, "I thought..."

She takes a step forward and regards him more closely now, her face a sweet mask. "You thought what?"

"I thought... that you were an angel." It doesn't sound all that strange. She waits for more. He notices the faintest shade of amber still lingering about the corona of her curls. "My angel," he adds.

She does not scream. Or laugh. Or slap his face. She simply nods and says, "Your angel? Oh, my."

Now that it's done, Stanley feels release deep in his bones, as though he's earned something by the sweat of his brow and now it's time to lay his burden down. Now he wants only to leave before something bad happens.

He clears his throat, says, "Excuse me," and backs up with a clumsy gesture of one arm and one leg, a little number we'll call "A Clown's Farewell."

Moving off, he misses the crooked little smile that infuses her features with a deeper light. When he hears her say, "Wait," he stops, startled to the bottom of his soul. A quiet moment passes before she says, "What's your name?"

DR. DANIEL BLACK

Miss Loretha's Last Stand

PEEKING FROM BEHIND THE GREEN, DISCOLORED, VELVET living room drapes as though someone were watching her, Miss Loretha released the edges slowly and resumed her seat in a nearby rocker. She was 79—80 in October—and had not been outside in weeks. She felt pretty good, she told her daughter morning and evening, but she wouldn't risk it. She didn't trust that virus. Too many folks 'cross the water had died, and a few folks right here were sick, too. Science people on TV warned old folks to stay away from other folks, especially if they had preexisting conditions. "Hell," she mumbled at the TV. "Who gets old without 'em?"

Most days, she'd rise with the sun and brew her morning coffee as she listened to *Good Morning America*. The pandemic was on the loose. That was all they ever said. Miss Loretha believed it was in the air, although they didn't say this. Newscasters didn't say a lotta things that were true. She wondered how in the world Trump had avoided the disease, especially since he went everywhere and never did wear a mask. *Probably got a vaccine for white folks already*, she thought. *Wouldn't surprise me.*

With a second cup in hand, she'd shuffle to the living room and plant herself in the rocker she'd bought for Stanley over 20 years before. *My Stanley*, she called him even now, as though she'd literally created him. He'd died 22 years earlier—August 2, 1998—in that very chair where she'd thought he'd simply fallen asleep. After calling him to bed and getting no response, she'd known he was gone. Their routine had included this beckoning, plus his murmured frustration as he'd struggled upward from the tattered recliner and stomped into the bedroom, falling asleep again before she could initiate the delightful exchange she'd always dreamed of. That night, when she'd called his name sweetly—*Stanley? Honey?*—and he hadn't roused, she'd smiled over the kitchen sink and thanked God for the years they'd shared. The time had not been perfect by any imagination— he'd had other women, she was sure—but he'd always come home at night, and that was more than most women could say.

Instead of calling an ambulance right away, she'd waited. She'd studied his face, his posture, his rounded, protruding belly, and re- membered the man she'd fallen in love with. This hadn't been him. He'd been tall and debonair, dressed to the nines with a slender form she'd definitely preferred. Now, dead in the chair, he'd been thick and chubby and bloated in the face. He hadn't been unattractive, she'd thought. After all, both of them had seen better days. But he had let himself go over the years, and only then had she realized she hadn't loved him so much as she'd needed him.

She'd thought she'd lose her mind in that apartment all by her- self, but she hadn't. Years had gone by and she'd made a life, feeding the hungry at the church and taking care of grandkids during the summer. They'd soon grown into adults and stopped coming. Her only child, Janice, had moved north with a man whom she, Loretha, had never preferred, so they seldom visited, and now that she was old, she'd gotten skeptical of the outdoors.

But she'd not been downright afraid. Not like this. The pandemic had come suddenly, unannounced, frightening like a plague, the way frogs and locusts must've descended upon Egypt. In Miss Loretha's opinion, it had come to kill the righteous. *The old folks.* Those who had earned the right to sit and enjoy life. Now they spent their days hoping the invisible monster didn't get them.

She hadn't touched another's flesh in months. No one had even seen her. Her daughter had arranged for groceries to be delivered, and when they came, she waited several minutes before handling them, spraying the bags with Lysol and praying aloud to ensure that the virus never felt welcomed. The delivery boy always mashed the buzzer quickly, then left the bags inside the small foyer. He assumed the customer was an old lady because she never retrieved the bags right away. She was probably more afraid of him than the disease, he thought.

She hated eating the same foods over and over again, but restaurant delivery, with its insanely expensive pricing, was out of the question. She'd always been a decent cook, but her meals were normally interspersed with visits to Friday's or Olive Garden or Ruby Tuesday or Red Lobster. Janice had chuckled once, telling her parents that those weren't *real* restaurants, but Loretha had paid her no mind. They were as real as her money allowed, she'd said. Plus, food in those high-end places was never worth what they charged. "I mean, really." She'd smirked. "What can you do with a chicken breast to make it worth $50?"

For days, she tried new dishes that got old quickly. Baked chicken, smothered chicken, barbequed chicken, chicken and dumplings, stir-fried chicken, chicken parmesan, you name it. Pork and beef had been abandoned years before, per doctor's orders, and only then had she ever reconsidered them. She needed something new. Or something *else*. She'd never liked fish, although Stanley had, but she enjoyed other seafood. The problem was that she'd never cooked it. And when she tried, it didn't turn out well. She didn't understand that *blackened* didn't mean *burnt*.

There were only so many vegetables she knew. Having migrated from the South in the '50s—then back in the '70s—she'd never heard of asparagus or eggplant or artichoke. Over the years, she'd tried them at dinner parties or the few upscale restaurants she'd experienced, but never had they become part of her everyday diet. What she ate was cabbage and greens and black-eyed peas and green beans. Poor people's vegetables. Now she was sick of them all.

Each day, Loretha stood at her living room window and stole glances at an abandoned world. Where streets had used to be loud and bustling with children, they were now silent, as though the apocalypse had come. A few stray people hurried along, but for the most part, everyone, like her, had gone underground. If not for TV, she could've been convinced that the world had come to an end. Actually, in the ways she knew it, it had.

She'd never had cable, although when her grandkids had been young, they had *put her on* to Apple TV. That was the phrase they'd used. It had sounded funny—"put her on"—like someone had been signing her up for some volunteer effort, but, in the end, she'd liked it. The phrase and the access to TV. She'd liked most watching Netflix on a big screen instead of that small-screened laptop her daughter had insisted she'd needed although she hadn't. Miss Loretha had resisted all forms of social media, believing technology to be to blame for the destruction of modern education and the depth of human interaction. If she were going to write a letter, she'd take the time to do that, she thought, in real penmanship, the way a letter ought to be written. Otherwise, she'd call. She saw no merit in useless, senseless Facebook messages, which conveyed little more than arbitrary thoughts and personal actions about which she couldn't have cared less.

Yet she had to admit that the Apple TV came in handy. For hours on end, once she'd read her Bible verses and cleaned whichever room she hadn't cleaned the day before, she'd sit and read movie titles until finding something that, hopefully, wouldn't disturb her conservative sensibilities. Comedies were her favorite, but the stand-up movies were so vulgar as to be unwatchable. And many of the movies, especially the Jim-Carrey-types, were simply stupid and unintelligent. Still she searched, watching the beginnings of movie after movie, until settling, day after day, for the blaxploitation genre of the 1970s. *Cotton Comes to Harlem, Let's Do It Again,* and *Uptown Saturday Night* restored her sanity each evening after watching stories of death and fear on CBS News. They warned old folks to "stay put," or, as the CDC said it, "quarantine in place." Loretha hadn't taken it seriously until people over 70 had started dropping like flies. Hospitals didn't have enough rooms; mortuaries couldn't accommodate the demand. Then her friend upstairs had gotten it and couldn't get any help. Health officials had told her to ride it out. They'd come and test her when more test kits arrived. What she'd ridden out had been a gurney two weeks later. Loretha had spoken to her every day, trying to keep her encouraged and hopeful, but day by day, she'd heard her friend's spirit diminish until, one day, Loretha had called and gotten no answer. She hadn't wanted to think the worst, but what else was there to think?

That had been the day she'd barricaded herself inside.

"Hello? Janice?" she'd whispered, as though the virus were listening and might've been offended.

"Momma? Is that you? Why you talkin' so low?"

Loretha had cleared her throat but hadn't increased her volume. "I'm not letting anyone else inside. Not now. Not for a while."

Janice had heard the fear. "Okay, Momma, but you're gonna be all right. You gotta at least go out for food and—"

"No!" she'd shouted as though Janice had not been listening. "I'm not leaving here for any reason."

"You don't have to be so scared, Momma. Plenty people get COVID-19 and survive it."

"Are those people 80?"

Janice had sighed. "Well, at least let me set up a grocery delivery service so you have food every day."

Loretha hadn't objected.

Janice had still heard fear in her mother's silence. "Try not to worry, Mom. You'll be okay. I'll be up soon's I can."

Loretha had lain the receiver on the base before saying goodbye. She'd needed to send a message to the church, too; otherwise, deacons and missionaries would be knocking on her door before long. And they wouldn't get it. She'd thought of the mail and decided she didn't care. Most of it was junk, anyway. She paid her bills over the phone. So, yes, she could avoid the world for a few weeks.

Weeks had turned into months. Each day, she'd listened as Fauci had described the virus's deadly behavior. The only guarantee against it, officials had said, was isolation, so that was what she'd done. But she wished someone had told her that loneliness killed, too.

By the fourth month, she woke and realized the distance between the kitchen and the living room had shrunk. Pausing for a moment, she looked in both directions, knowing full well she'd lived there over 20 years and could've walked the short pathway blindfolded. Yet suddenly it was different. At least it felt different. She paced it again and again, counting the steps from one room to the other, and she knew something had changed. It frightened her. It surprised her. This sudden minimalizing confirmed what she already knew: she couldn't stay in that apartment alone forever. Not forever *and ever.*

She thought she might be losing her mind, the way her Stanley had begun to, but then she remembered who she was, where she was, what her name was, so she stopped worrying. She got her Bible and read aloud the 23rd Psalm: "The Lord is my shepherd, I shall not want!" She stood suddenly and moved about the small space, reading aloud and touching things as though anointing them. When she got to "Yea though I walk through the valley of the shadow of death," she laid her trembling left hand upon her chest and began to cry. "Thou preparest a table before me in the presence of my enemies." That was how she thought of the virus: as an enemy lurking in the streets, determined to find and destroy her. It was alive and conscious, omnipotent even, strategizing an assault upon a black widow who had decided to live. Yet it could not come without her permission, her willingness to welcome it. And Loretha Mae Johnson was not willing.

At first, it had seemed to choke only white people. In fact, some had thought black people might be immune. But Loretha knew better. Anything white people had, black people soon got, so it was only a matter of time. And when black people got it, it seemed angrier, even offended, perhaps, that black people had thought they were off the hook. It destroyed more thoroughly, as though to put black people back in their places. But not Loretha. She was ready. She and God had seen it coming, so after the second day of quarantining herself inside, Loretha had taken a little blood from a chicken she'd cut up and marked a tiny "X" on her front door. Now the virus knew to skip over her place in its silent rampage.

For months she'd sat, praying and reading and watching Sidney Poitier. He was the tone of chocolate she liked, the same complexion her Stanley had been. No man had touched her since his death, but sometimes she longed for it. She would never have told a living soul that, once, she'd touched herself as Poitier's piercing eyes had watched her from the TV screen. She hadn't known that a woman's touch, let alone her own, could elicit an ecstasy so marvelous that it caused her to tremble, but that was precisely what had happened. She'd never done it again. She didn't want to go to Hell for adultery when Heaven was within reach.

After the fifth month, the apartment was so small she could hardly move about. None of her clothes fit anymore. They'd shrunk to the size she'd been before the pandemic. All the movies she liked, she'd seen multiple times. Even the Bible had begun to bore her, although she fought that truth for fear of God's disappointment. The mark of blood on her door had worked. The evil thing had not gotten her.

Or had it?

She knew what to do. The answer, like a logical conclusion, hit her one Tuesday evening as she watched young people on TV protest the death of George Floyd. They had gotten out of hand, these police shootings of black men, and Loretha felt proud that, finally, black people were showing out. She hated that, by simply being together, they were putting themselves in harm's way, but she understood their behavior as their clarity that something was worth dying for.

At 10 a.m. the next morning, dressed in a cool, floral-patterned summer dress and straw hat, Loretha stood at her front door with an unsteady hand clutched to the knob and blinked back tears of uncertainty. This could cost her everything. It would definitely cost her *something*. But it had to be done. Her apartment had squeezed the life out of her when she'd thought that, by staying inside, she'd avoided death.

So Loretha looked around one last time. She apologized to Stanley, her Stanley, for her infidelity and told him it had only been because she'd missed him so. She felt forgiven. She sighed. Then she turned the knob, opened the door, and breathed deeply.

Contributors

JUDY FARRINGTON AUST is a longtime Georgia resident who has made her home in Tucker, just outside Atlanta, for thirty-five years. Throughout her life, Judy has explored various creative arts, including music, visual art, and the written word. Five years ago, at the encouragement of a friend who is a published author, she started writing fiction, and she now has a novel in the works with the hope of one day getting to the end. In the meantime, she is an attorney, practicing litigation and mediation in Atlanta and beyond.

DR. DANIEL BLACK is an award-winning novelist, professor, and activist. His published works include *They Tell Me of Home*, *The Sacred Place*, *Perfect Peace*, *Twelve Gates to the City*, *The Coming*, and *Listen to the Lambs*. In 2014, he won the Distinguished Writer's Award from the Mid-Atlantic Writer's Association. The Go On Girl! National Book Club named him "Author of the Year" in 2011 for his novel *Perfect Peace*. *Perfect Peace* was also chosen as the 2014 selection for "If All Arkansas Read the Same Book" by the Arkansas Center for the Book at the Arkansas State Library. Dr. Black has also been nominated for the Townsend Literary Prize, Ernest J. Gaines Award, Ferro-Grumbley Literary Prize, Lambda Literary Award, and Georgia Author of the Year Prize. Dr. Black works intermittently as a diversity consultant, having spoken at top-tier companies in America, such as Google and Chan Zuckerberg Initiative. A native of Kansas City, Kansas, Dr. Black spent his formative years in rural Blackwell, Arkansas. Dr. Black graduated from Clark College (now Clark Atlanta University), where he earned the prestigious Oxford Modern British Studies fellowship and studied at Oxford University. He was awarded a full fellowship to Temple University, where he studied with poet laureate of the Black Arts Movement Sonia Sanchez and earned his Ph.D. in African-American Studies. Dr. Black is Professor of African-American Studies at his alma mater, Clark Atlanta University. Dr. Black lives in Atlanta and is the founder of the Ndugu-Nzinga Rites of Passage Nation, a mentoring society for African-American youth.

A longtime resident of Atlanta and a member of the Atlanta Writers Club for many years, **MARGARET ELIZABETH BROOK** is a graduate of Columbia University. She freely admits her life is ruled by a Cavalier King Charles Spaniel named Wesley. She writes poetry and historical fiction and is currently seeking representation for her novel, *An Ocean of Blame*, which is based on the life of Titanic Lookout Frederick Fleet.

RICKI CARDENAS is the author of two humorous women's fiction novels, *Mr. Right-Swipe* and *Switch and Bait* (Grand Central, 2017 and 2018). She earned a B.A. in English and an M.Ed. in Secondary Education from John Carroll University in Cleveland, Ohio—and she's molded the minds of tweens and teens as a middle school and high school English teacher both there and in Atlanta. She currently lives in Marietta with her husband and two crazy beagles, and she's finally starting to embrace "y'all"—even though she can't pull it off even a little bit. Visit her on the web: *rickicardenas.com*; *facebook.com/rickicardibooks* (Facebook); *instagram.com/rickicardibooks* (Instagram); and @RickiCardi (Twitter).

EMILY CARPENTER is the critically acclaimed, bestselling author of suspense novels *Burying the Honeysuckle Girls*, *The Weight of Lies*, *Every Single Secret*, *Until the Day I Die*, and her most recent release, *Reviving the Hawthorn Sisters*, published by Lake Union. After graduating from Auburn with a Bachelor of Arts in Speech Communication, she moved to New York City. She's worked as an actor, producer, screenwriter, and behind-the-scenes soap opera assistant for the CBS shows *As the World Turns* and *Guiding Light*.

Born and raised in Birmingham, Alabama, she now lives in Atlanta, Georgia, with her family. You can visit Emily at *emilycarpenterauthor. com* and on Facebook and Twitter and Instagram.

AMY COX is a Speech-Language Pathologist in Flowery Branch, GA. She received a B.S.Ed. from the University of Georgia and M.A. from The University of Memphis. She has been married to her high school sweetheart for 22 years and has two teenaged daughters. Amy is a member of the Atlanta Writers Club and develops therapy products for Speech-Language Pathologists.

GINGER EAGER'S 2020 debut novel, *The Nature of Remains*, won The AWP Prize for the Novel. Her short stories, essays, and reviews have appeared in various online and print journals. Born and raised in Georgia, Ginger now lives in Decatur with her husband and their cats. Find her online at *www.gingereager.com*.

ANJALI ENJETI is an award-winning journalist and activist. Her debut novel, *The Parted Earth*, is forthcoming from Hub City Press, and her essay collection about identity and activism is forthcoming from UGA Press. Her work has appeared in the *Paris Review, The Atlanta Journal-Constitution, The Washington Post, Newsday,* and elsewhere. She teaches creative nonfiction in the MFA program at Reinhardt University in Waleska, Georgia.

DAVID FULMER is the author of twelve works of fiction, including the award-winning and critically-acclaimed Storyville series. He is currently working on his thirteenth novel, *The Book of Secrets*. He lives in Atlanta with his wife, Sansanee Sermprungsuk.

HOLLIS GILLESPIE is an award-winning humor writer, best-selling author, travel columnist, NPR commentator, and travel expert for NBC's *Today* and *The Dr. Oz Show*, which is syndicated by Sony Television. Following the release of her first book, Hollis was a guest on *The Tonight Show* with Jay Leno

("A very funny lady," says Leno). She began her career writing feature and investigative pieces for Atlanta's *Creative Loafing* newspaper, then the fourth largest alternative publication in the nation. Her celebrated humor column garnered her the title of "Atlanta's Best Columnist" seven out of the next eight years. Gillespie founded the Shocking Real Life Writing Academy in 2007. Since then, it has grown into the largest independent writing school in the Southeast. Gillespie's work has been optioned by Sony Pictures and Paramount, and she has collaborated with Hollywood hard hitters like Mitch Hurwitz, the creator of *Arrested Development*, Eric and Kim Tannenbaum, producers of *Two and a Half Men*, and Amy Palladino, creator of *Gilmore Girls*. *Kirkus Reviews* lauded Gillespie's "impeccable comic timing" for her first novel, titled *Unaccompanied Minor* ("A laugh-out-loud thriller about family court, money laundering and skyjacking"). For the same novel, *Booklist* heralded Gillespie as "a fantastic narrator: smart, funny, angry, and gifted in sarcasm." Her fifth novel, titled *We Will Be Crashing Shortly*, was released in 2015.

Named the "Funniest Woman in Georgia" by *Southern Living Magazine*, **LAURETTA HANNON** is the author of *The Cracker Queen—A Memoir of a Jagged, Joyful Life* (Gotham Books, Penguin) and has been a commentator on National Public Radio's *All Things Considered*, where her stories have reached 25 million listeners. Lauretta is in-demand as a keynote speaker and offers writing and self-growth seminars as well as one-on-one consultations for writers. She writes in a shed that was once the site of a covert moonshining operation. This pleases her to no end.

MARIN HENRY is a metro Atlanta native who was raised in Lilburn, Georgia. Although her background is in foreign language education, she still greatly enjoys writing fiction, nonfiction, and poetry. In her free time, you can find her dabbling in all sorts of activities, from playing the violin to hiking nature trails. "Group Therapy" is her very first publication. She hopes to one day have a career in writing and start a successful blog. She says, "I love writing and have always felt that it has given me a voice. I am beyond humbled that someone would care about what I have to say."

ROGER JOHNS is the author of the Wallace Hartman Mysteries, *Dark River Rising* and *River of Secrets*, from St. Martin's Press/Minotaur Books. He is the 2018 Georgia Author of the Year (Detective-Mystery Category), a two-time Killer Nashville Silver Falchion Award Finalist, and runner-up for the 2019 Frank Yerby Fiction Award. Roger's articles and interviews about writing and career management for new authors have appeared in *Criminal Element*, *Career Authors*, the *Southern Literary Review*, *Writer Unboxed*, and *Southern Writers Magazine*. He is a member of the Atlanta Writers Club, Mystery Writers of America, International Thriller Writers, and Sisters in Crime. Along with several other writers, he co-authors the MurderBooks blog at *www.murder-books.com*. Visit him at: *www.rogerjohnsbooks.com*.

SONIAH KAMAL is an award-winning novelist, essayist and public speaker. Her novel, *Unmarriageable: Pride & Prejudice in Pakistan* is featured on PBS Books. *Publishers Weekly*'s starred review hails it a "must read for devout Austenites," and *Shelf Awareness*'s starred review says that "If Jane Austen lived in modern-day Pakistan, this is the version of *Pride and Prejudice* she might have written." Accolades for *Unmarriageable* include a *Financial Times* Readers' Best Book of 2019, an NPR's *Code Switch* and New York Public Library 2019 Summer Read Pick, a *People* Magazine Pick, a *Library Journal* starred review and Library Reads Pick, a 2019 "Books All Georgians Should Read," a nominee for the 2020 Georgia Author of the Year for Literary Fiction, a shortlisting for the 2020 Townsend Award for Fiction, and more. Soniah's novel *An Isolated Incident* was a finalist for the Townsend Award for Fiction and the KLF French Fiction Prize and an Amazon Rising Star Pick. Soniah's work has appeared in critically acclaimed anthologies and publications, including *The*

New York Times, The Guardian, the TEDX stage, *The Georgia Review, Bitter Southerner, Catapult*, and more. She is on Twitter and Instagram @soniahkamal.

A 2006 inductee into the Georgia Writers Hall of Fame and a 2009 recipient of the Governor's Award in the Humanities, **TERRY KAY** is the author of the southern classic *To Dance with the White Dog* and 17 other published works, including fiction, essays, and children's books as well as screenplays. A four-time recipient of the Author of the Year Award in Georgia, three of Kay's novels have been produced as Hallmark Hall of Fame movies. He has also been awarded the Townsend Award, the Lindberg Award, and the Appalachian Heritage Award. The Atlanta Writers Club's annual award for fiction is named the Terry Kay Prize for Fiction. LaGrange College and Mercer University have recognized his work with honorary doctorate degrees.

DEVI S. LASKAR is a native of Chapel Hill, North Carolina, and holds an MFA from Columbia University. *The Atlas of Reds and Blues*—winner of the Asian/Pacific American Award for Literature and the Crook's Corner Book Prize—is her first novel. It was selected by The Georgia Center for the Book as a book "All Georgians Should Read," longlisted for the DSC Prize in South Asian Literature, and longlisted for the Golden Poppy Award presented by the California Independent Booksellers Alliance.

MAN MARTIN is a three-time winner of Georgia Author of the Year from the Georgia Writers Association and a finalist for the 2018 Townsend Prize for his novel, *The Lemon Jell-O Syndrome*. His daily cartoon, "Man Overboard," appears online and through email subscription and can been seen on Facebook as "Man Overboard Cartoons." He lives in Atlanta with his wife Nancy, where he divides his time equally between writing, cartooning, and raising chickens.

TERRA ELAN MCVOY is the author of eight novels for young people, including *This is All Your Fault, Cassie Parker*, from HarperCollins, and the Edgar Award finalist *Criminal*, from Simon & Schuster. Most of her jobs have focused on reading and writing, including being manager of Little Shop of Stories, program director for the AJC Decatur Book Festival, and answering fan mail for Captain Underpants while an editorial assistant at Scholastic. Her master's degree is from Florida State University in Creative Writing, and she has taught both adults and young people in a variety of courses, including the Yale Writers Workshop and Smith College Young Women's Writing Workshop, among others. You can learn more about Terra and her books at *http://terraelan.com*.

ELIZABETH MUSSER, an Atlanta native, writes "entertainment with a soul" from her writing chalet—tool shed—outside Lyon, France. Elizabeth's highly acclaimed, bestselling novel *The Swan House* was named one of Amazon's Top Christian Books of the Year and one of Georgia's Top Ten Novels of the Past 100 Years. All of Elizabeth's novels have been translated into multiple languages and have been international bestsellers. Find more about Elizabeth's novels at *www.elizabethmusser.com* and on Facebook, Instagram, Twitter, and her blog (*elizabethmusser.wordpress.com*).

SCOTT THOMAS OUTLAR lives and writes in the suburbs outside of Atlanta, Georgia. His work has been nominated for the Pushcart Prize and Best of the Net. He guest-edited the 2019 and 2020 Western Voices editions of *Setu Mag*. Selections of his poetry have been translated into Afrikaans, Albanian, Bengali, Dutch, French, Italian, Kurdish, Persian, Serbian, and Spanish. His sixth book, *Of Sand and Sugar*, was released in 2019 through Cyberwit Press. His podcast, *Songs of Selah*, airs weekly on 17Numa Radio and features interviews with contemporary poets, artists, musicians, and health advocates. More about Outlar's work can be found at *17Numa.com*.

GWYNDOLYN D. PARKER, a business and community leader during a long career, was recognized with the 1999 "25 Most Influential Black Women in Business" Award by *The Network Journal*, a Volunteer of the Year Award in Allentown, PA, and a Citation from the State of Pennsylvania Senate and House of Representatives for receiving the 2008 YWCA Racial Justice Award, among other recognitions. She was involved in a range of initiatives and organizations that worked for green issues, educational improvement, social justice, diversity, and racial equity. She retired in 2008, moved to Douglasville, GA, and began a new career as a writer. Between 2010 and 2019, she self-published 11 books, from *It's Hard to Catch Fall – Except Through the Rearview Mirror* (2010) to *The Re-Knowing Revisited* (2019). She is a member of the Atlanta Writers Club. In addition to her writing in retirement, she also started Up By the Bootstraps, Inc. to help students succeed. Her motto is "If you are so privileged to see a need, do something about it, for God opens eyes that have the ability to act on what they see."

CLAYTON H. RAMSEY, an Atlanta native and ninth-generation Georgian, is a former two-term president of the Atlanta Writers Club and current Officer Emeritus and VP of Contests, Awards & Scholarships. With degrees from Princeton and Emory, he is a regular contributor to *Georgia Backroads* magazine and has also been published in *The Writer, The Chattahoochee Review, The Blue Mountain Review, Mash Stories,* and others. He has appeared on Georgia Public Broadcasting and National Public Radio, served on the Townsend Prize for Fiction selection committee, and been honored for his work by *The Writer*, the Georgia Writers Museum, and the Atlanta Writers Club. He lives in Decatur with his wife.

WILLIAM RAWLINGS is a sixth-generation resident of Washington County, Georgia. A retired physician, he is an avid world traveler, photographer, and prolific writer, including six novels and four works of nonfiction focusing on Southern history. His most recent book, *Six Inches Deeper*, was released by Mercer University

Press in March 2020. An eleventh nonfiction work on lighthouses of the Georgia coast is scheduled for publication in early 2021. For more information, please visit his website at *www.williamrawlings.com*.

JANISSE RAY is an American writer whose subject is often nature. She is author of five books of literary nonfiction and a volume of eco-poetry. She holds an MFA from the University of Montana, where she was the William Kittredge Distinguished Visiting Writer in 2014. She is a 2015 inductee into the Georgia Writers Hall of Fame. She won the 2017 Southern Environmental Law Center Award in journalism for her piece on coal ash, published in *The Bitter Southerner*. In 2018, she was the Louis D. Rubin Jr. Writer-in-Residence at Hollins University in Roanoke, VA, and in 2019, she won the Georgia Author of the Year Lifetime Achievement Award from the Georgia Writers Association. Her first book, *Ecology of a Cracker Childhood*, is a memoir about growing up on a junkyard in the ruined longleaf pine ecosystem of the Southeast. It was a *New York Times* Notable Book and was chosen as the Book All Georgians Should Read. Ray's most recent book, *The Seed Underground: A Growing Revolution to Save Food*, looks at heirloom seeds. The book has been translated into Turkish and French and has won numerous awards. The author was born in southern Georgia, where she returned to live on an organic farm near the confluence of the Altamaha and Ohoopee rivers.

A longtime Atlantan originally from New Orleans, **NEDRA PEZOLD ROBERTS** swapped teaching drama and English at The Westminster Schools for writing her own plays. Over the past several years, she has had production runs or staged readings coast to coast, and in Canada and the UK. Many of the plays have been published and/or have won competitions. Nedra is a former AWC board member and for years ran the creative writing contests, and she still helps with the writing conferences. She was honored in 2019 as AWC's inaugural Member of the Year.

NICKI SALCEDO is the author of *All Beautiful Things* and three essay collections. Her writing often appears on *Decaturish.com*. She works in the corporate world by day and writes at night. She lives in Atlanta with her husband, four kids, and three cats. She can be found online at *nickisalcedo.com*.

A self-described late bloomer, **SUSAN SANDS** began writing her first novel at age forty. She describes her challenging journey to publication as "raising another child—a difficult one." Susan has published five southern, contemporary women's fiction novels set in Alabama. She describes her humorous small-town stories as fun, romantic, and filled with big family love. Susan has three grown children and lives with her dentist husband in Johns Creek, GA. She is a member of the Georgia Romance Writers, the Romance Writers of America, the Atlanta Writers Club, and the Broadleaf Writers Association. She participates in book festivals, book clubs, and writers' conferences around the South. Susan is the recipient of the 2017 Georgia Author of the Year award for romance.

A former music journalist, **ANNA SCHACHNER** has published short fiction and nonfiction in many journals and magazines, including *Puerto del Sol, Ontario Review,* and *The Sun,* and she contributes nonfiction about books and literary culture to publications such as *The Guardian* and *The Atlanta Journal-Constitution. You and I and Someone Else,* her first novel and a finalist for the Foreword Indies Book of the Year award and the Georgia Author of the Year award, was released by Mercer University Press in April 2017. She directs Georgia's Townsend Prize for Fiction and volunteers with Reforming Arts to teach writing in the Georgia prison system. She lives in Atlanta, where she is the editor of *The Chattahoochee Review.* Visit her at *annaschachner.com*.

JEDWIN SMITH has battled malaria and evaded Soviet and Ethiopian soldiers to become a 1986 Pulitzer Prize finalist for his war coverage in East Africa, plus earning a Pulitzer nomination for his war coverage in Beirut, Lebanon, in 1983-84. He's compared battle scars with great motorcycle daredevil Evel Knievel and had a near-death experience bringing Spanish gold, silver, and emeralds to the surface from the fabled galleon *Atocha*. He is the author of *Our Brother's Keeper, Let's Get It On! The Mills Lane Story*, and *Fatal Treasure. I AM ISRAEL—Lions and Lambs of the Land* was released in 2018 from Blue Room Books.

WILLIAM WALSH is the director of the Reinhardt University M.F.A. program and a southern narrative poet in the tradition of James Dickey, David Bottoms, and Fred Chappell. In 2020, his new collection of poems, *Fly Fishing in Times Square*, was published by Červená Barva Press (Boston), which had recently won the Editors' Prize. His novels *The Boomerang Mattress* and *Haircuts for the Dead* were Finalists and Semi-Finalists in the William Faulkner Pirate Alley Prize. As well, his novel, *The Pig Rider*, was Finalist in 2015. His other books include: *Speak So I Shall Know Thee: Interviews with Southern Writers* (McFarland, 1990); *The Ordinary Life of a Sculptor* (Sandstone, 1993); *The Conscience of My Other Being* (Cherokee Publishers, 2005); *Under the Rock Umbrella: Contemporary American Poets from 1951-1977* (Mercer, 2006); *David Bottoms: Critical Essays and Interviews* (McFarland, 2010), and *Lost In the White Ruins* (2014). His work has also appeared in a number of distinguished literary journals.

GEORGE WEINSTEIN is the author of the Southern historical novel *Hardscrabble Road*, the novel of forgotten U.S. history *The Five Destinies of Carlos Moreno*, the contemporary romance *The Caretaker*, the Southern mystery *Aftermath*, and the suspense thriller *Watch What You Say*. George is the Executive Director and Acting President of the Atlanta Writers Club and has helped thousands of writers on their quest for publication through the Club and the twice-yearly Atlanta Writers Conference, which he has managed for more than ten years.

TARA WHITE is an architectural lighting designer and member of the Illuminating Engineering Society. She graduated from Yale University with a bachelor's degree in Art History and from the Rhode Island School of Design with a master's degree in Interior Architecture. At RISD, she studied abroad in Russia and Japan, was one of the winners of the Annual English Department Fiction Competition, and had a nonfiction article published in the *form-Z Joint Study Journal*. Tara lives in Johns Creek and loves cats, cooking, textiles, and walking the paths along the Chattahoochee River.

Share Your Thoughts

Want to help make *Viral Literature* a bestselling book? Consider leaving an honest review of this book on Goodreads, on your personal author website or blog, and anywhere else readers go for recommendations. It's our priority at SFK Press to publish books for readers to enjoy, and our authors appreciate and value your feedback.

Our Southern Fried Guarantee

If you wouldn't enthusiastically recommend one of our books with a 4- or 5-star rating to a friend, then the next story is on us. We believe that much in the stories we're telling. Simply email us at pr@sfkmultimedia.com.

Do You Know About Our Bi-Monthly Zine?

Would you like your unpublished prose, poetry, or visual art featured in *The New Southern Fugitives*? A bi-monthly zine that's free to readers and subscribers *and* pays contributors:

$100 for essays and short stories
$50 for book reviews
$40 for flash/micro fiction
$40 for poetry
$40 for photography & visual art

Visit **NewSouthernFugitives.com/**
Submit for more information.

Also Available from SFK Press

A Body's Just as Dead by Cathy Adams
Not All Migrate by Krystyna Byers
The Banshee of Machrae by Sonja Condit
Amidst This Fading Light by Rebecca Davis
American Judas by Mickey Dubrow
Swapping Purples for Yellows by Matthew Duffus
A Curious Matter of Men with Wings by F. Rutledge Hammes
The Skin Artist by George Hovis
Saint Catastrophe by Sarah Jilek
Lying for a Living by Steve McCondichie
The Parlor Girl's Guide by Steve McCondichie
Appalachian Book of the Dead by Dale Neal
Feral, North Carolina, 1965 by June Sylvester Saraceno
If Darkness Takes Us by Brenda Marie Smith
The Escape to Candyland by Yong Takahashi
Aftermath by George Weinstein
Hardscrabble Road by George Weinstein
The Caretaker by George Weinstein
The Five Destinies of Carlos Moreno by George Weinstein
Watch What You Say by George Weinstein
RIPPLES by Evan Williams

Forthcoming from SFK Press in Spring 2021
Falling by Rebekah Coxwell
Red Door Scriptures by Brenda Wilson

From Hearthstone Press

Sanctuary: A Legacy of Memories by T.M. Brown
Testament: An Unexpected Return by T.M. Brown
Purgatory: A Progeny's Quest by T.M. Brown
Tallapoosa: A Southern Novel by Mike Corwin
Ariel's Island by Pat McKee
Paper & Ink, Flesh & Blood by Rita Mace Walston

Forthcoming from Hearthstone Press in Spring 2021
Tidewater Tempest by M.Z. Thwaite

From Brown Chicken Books

Lacrimosa (Shadows of the Mind: Book One) by Mandi Jourdan

Forthcoming from Brown Chicken Books in Spring 2021
MotherLove by Janet Chapman
Parker's Choice by Michael Nemeth

From Blissful Beings

Throwing It All Away: A Son's Suicide and a Mother's Search for Hope by Nina Owen

Forthcoming from Blissful Beings in Spring 2021
Unconditioned Love by Staci Diffendaffer
Declaration of Interdependence by Lisa Uhrik

Made in the USA
Columbia, SC
03 December 2020